What people are saying about …

# Erasing Hell

"*Erasing Hell* is an extraordinarily important book. Francis Chan speaks with trembling and compassion. He recognizes this debate is about God, His nature, and His authority. At stake is whether or not we will trust Him. Francis lays his heart on the table; I was not only informed, but moved. It's rare that a book mixes straight-from-the-heart talk with diligent citation of Scripture. *Erasing Hell* is highly readable yet goes deep and into detail exactly when it needs to. Preston Sprinkle's research and Francis Chan's presentation are a dynamic combination. This remarkable book embraces not what, in pride, we want to believe, but what, in humility, we must believe. My heartfelt thanks to Francis Chan for taking us to God's Word in a Christlike spirit of grace and truth. And for calling on us not to apologize for God, but to apologize *to* God for presuming to be wiser and more loving than our Savior."

**Randy Alcorn,** author of *Heaven*
and *If God Is Good*

"It's time for the H word. A lot of people go through hell on earth, but what if there is also a hell *after* earth? Hell's stock has fallen off lately from lack of public confidence, but how can thousands, perhaps millions, reject hell as a myth and yet still believe in heaven and cherish fond hopes of going there? Surely if we hate suffering,

God must hate it worse and could never have founded an institution as horrible as described in Dante's *Inferno*. But the same Jesus who gave heaven a five-star rating also described an otherworldly chamber of horrors. Who goes there and why? And for how long? In *Erasing Hell,* my good friend Francis Chan takes a close look at some tough, frightening questions … and his answers may honestly surprise you!"

**Joni Eareckson Tada,** Joni and Friends
International Disability Center

"Everyone needs to read *Erasing Hell* by Francis Chan and Preston Sprinkle. Chan and Sprinkle accurately and clearly reflect the biblical teaching on heaven, hell, and eternal destiny. They provide a timely reminder that we don't define God, but He reveals Himself to us in the pages of Scripture."

**Tremper Longman,** Robert H. Gundry Professor
of Biblical Studies at Westmont College and
author of *Reading the Bible with Heart and Mind*

"Francis Chan and Preston Sprinkle raise the questions we all have about this very critical topic and respond with biblical integrity and a commitment to truth, as well as incredible compassion for people. *Erasing Hell* is an extremely important and much-needed book."

**Dan Kimball,** pastor and author of
*They Like Jesus but Not the Church*

"Francis holds the fine line between committed biblical faithfulness and a deep compassion for people and refuses to create a false dichotomy between the two. He feels the weight and horror of the reality of hell and yet avoids the error of lapsing into mere humanism, all the while providing a well-reasoned defense for the view of Scripture on the subject. I am so thankful for this book, as will you be."

**Britt Merrick,** pastor of Reality Santa Barbara

"Recent works by evangelicals on the postmortem future(s) of humanity have raised important questions and brought some sobering and uncomfortable issues to the fore. Chan and Sprinkle provide a remarkable service to the church by engaging these issues with courage, clarity, and grace. This book is a model of careful biblical scholarship, providing fresh light from the Jewish context of the New Testament. They also write as pastors seeking to provide wisdom for ministry, enabling the people of God to embody the love of God for the world."

**Timothy Gombis,** associate professor of New Testament at Grand Rapids Theological Seminary

# erasinghell

# erasinghell

what God said
about eternity, and the
things we made up

**francis chan
& preston sprinkle**

David C Cook®
*transforming lives together*

ERASING HELL
Published by David C Cook
4050 Lee Vance View
Colorado Springs, CO 80918 U.S.A.

David C Cook Distribution Canada
55 Woodslee Avenue, Paris, Ontario, Canada N3L 3E5

David C Cook U.K., Kingsway Communications
Eastbourne, East Sussex BN23 6NT, England

David C Cook and the graphic circle C logo
are registered trademarks of Cook Communications Ministries.

Unless otherwise noted, all Scripture quotations are taken from *The Holy Bible, English Standard Version.* Copyright © 2000; 2001 by Crossway Bibles, a division of Good News Publishers. Used by permission. All rights reserved. Scripture quotations marked NASB are taken from the *New American Standard Bible*, © Copyright 1960, 1995 by The Lockman Foundation. Used by permission. Scripture quotations marked NIV are taken from the Holy Bible, New International Version®, NIV®. Copyright © 1973, 1978, 1984 by Biblica, Inc™. Used by permission of Zondervan. All rights reserved worldwide. www.zondervan.com. Scripture marked TNIV taken from the HOLY BIBLE, TODAY'S NEW INTERNATIONAL VERSION®. Copyright © 2001, 2005 by Biblica®. Used by permission of Biblica®. All rights reserved worldwide. The author has added italics to Scripture and quotations for emphasis.

LCCN 2011929504
ISBN 978-0-7814-0725-0
eISBN 978-0-7814-0753-3

© 2011 Francis Chan and Preston Sprinkle
Published in association with the literary agency of
D.C. Jacobson & Associates LLC, an Author Management Company
www.dcjacobson.com

The Team: Don Pape, Alex Field, Amy Konyndyk, Nick Lee,
Caitlyn York, Renada Arens, Karen Athen
Cover Design: Jim Elliston, The Regime

Printed in the United States of America
First Edition 2011

1 2 3 4 5 6 7 8 9 10

052711

# Contents

# Preface

I wrote this book with my friend Preston. I recruited his help because he can interact with issues at a deeper level than I can. His expertise in language, history, and the New Testament has helped tremendously in our effort to be thorough and precise. Preston studied first-century Judaism for his doctorate and has published many works in this area. We thought it would be a good partnership because we have different gifts but similar convictions. As we wrote the book, we decided to write it with one voice (Francis's). Truth be told, the majority of research was done by Preston.

While Preston and I wrote this book, it could not have been completed without the meticulous help of many in our community.

First and foremost, Mark Beuving contributed many hours to editing, correcting, and rewriting sections with precision and care. Also, many staff at Eternity Bible College and Cornerstone Church in Simi Valley set aside precious hours to read through early drafts. Thank you, Joshua, Spencer, Yvonne, Todd, and Matt. Your comments were invaluable. I also solicited the help of many scholars, who combed through the book, or portions of it, to make sure my interpretations of Scripture were sound. These scholars include Dr. Timothy Gombis (Grand Rapids Theological Seminary), Dr. Tremper Longman III (Westmont College), Dr. Joseph Dodson (Ouachita Baptist University), Dr. Simon Gathercole (Cambridge University), and Dr. Scott Hafemann (St. Andrews University). Although I didn't intend this to be a "scholarly" book, its subject matter demanded the utmost caution in handling the biblical text. I am therefore grateful for the close inspection it received before going to print.

However, no matter how many human filters we solicited to purify the words of this book, it's still fallible. Because of this, we have included many direct quotes from Scripture. Read the Scriptures we've quoted as truth directly from the mouth of God. Pause and meditate deeply on the verses whenever they arise. Those words are ultimately what God wants you to cherish and embrace.

# Introduction

If you are excited to read this book, you have issues.

Do you understand the weight of what we are about to consider? We are exploring the possibility that you and I may end up being tormented in hell. *Excited* would be the wrong term to use here. *Necessary* would be more fitting.

For some, this discussion will open up old wounds. It certainly does for me.

The saddest day of my life was the day I watched my grandmother die. When that EKG monitor flatlined, I freaked out. I absolutely lost it! According to what I knew of the Bible, she was headed for a life of never-ending suffering. I thought I would go crazy. I have never cried harder, and I don't ever want to feel like that again. Since that day, I have tried not to think about it. It has been over twenty years.

Even as I write that paragraph, I feel sick. I would love to erase hell from the pages of Scripture.

How about you? Have you ever struggled with hell as I have? Do you have any parents, siblings, cousins, or friends who, based on what you have been taught, will end up in hell? What a bone-chilling thought. Until recently, whenever the idea of hell—and the idea of my loved ones possibly heading there—crossed my mind, I would brush it aside and divert my thinking to something more pleasant. While I've always believed in hell with my mind, I tried not to let the doctrine penetrate my heart.

But I reached a point where I could no longer do this. I could no longer acknowledge hell with my lips while preventing my heart from feeling its weight. I had to figure out if the Bible actually taught the existence of a literal hell. How great would it be if it *didn't?* Then I would be able to embrace my grandmother again someday.

So I decided to write a book about hell. And honestly—I'm scared to death.

I'm scared because so much is at stake. Think about it. If I say there is no hell, and it turns out that there is a hell, I may lead people into the very place I convinced them did not exist! If I say there is a hell, and I'm wrong, I may persuade people to spend their lives frantically warning loved ones about a terrifying place that isn't real! When it comes to hell, we can't afford to be wrong. This is not one of those doctrines where you can toss in your two cents, shrug your shoulders, and move on. Too much is at stake. Too many *people* are at stake. And the Bible has too much to say.

## Who Should I Believe?

Part of me doesn't *want* to believe in hell. And I'll admit that I have a tendency to read into Scripture what I want to find—maybe you do too. Knowing this, I've spent many hours fasting and praying that God would prevent my desires from twisting Scripture to gratify my personal preferences. And I encourage you to do the same. Don't believe something just because you want to, and don't embrace an idea just because you've always believed it. Believe what is biblical. Test all your assumptions against the precious words God gave us in the Bible.

There are many things that I believed and practiced for years, only to change my views after further study of the Bible. I've learned to be okay with saying, "I think I was off on that one." While this is humbling and difficult, it's better than continuing to believe something that is inaccurate.

For example, I was "initiated" into the American church when people urged me to pray a prayer to "receive Christ" so I wouldn't burn in hell. After years of leading others down the same path, I changed. I now speak against this idea of simply praying a prayer as fire insurance—I just don't see it anywhere in Scripture.

I was also taught that the Holy Spirit no longer empowers our lives with miraculous deeds, because these "ceased" long ago. For many years, I discouraged people from pursuing the supernatural.

After further study of Scripture, I now believe that the Spirit can heal the incurable, accomplish the impossible, and ignite believers to do greater works than Jesus (John 14:12). And I urge people to believe the same.

I have distanced myself from traditional forms of "church" in pursuit of what I believe is more biblical. I don't believe God wants our church life to be centered on buildings and services. Instead, God wants our churches—whatever specific forms our gatherings take—to be focused on active discipleship, mission, and the pursuit of unity.

At one point, I even sold my house, quit my job, and left the country because I didn't want any of my comforts to hold me back from pursuing God wholeheartedly. I wanted to follow God wherever He led me.

Why do I tell you all this?

*I'm not going to hang on to the idea of hell simply because it's what my tradition tells me to believe. And neither should you.*

Let's be eager to leave what is familiar for what is true. Nothing outside of God and His truth should be sacred to us. And so it is with hell. If hell is some primitive myth left over from conservative tradition, then let's set it on that dusty shelf next to other traditional beliefs that have no basis in Scripture. But if it is true, if the Bible does teach that there is a literal hell awaiting those who don't believe in Jesus, then this reality must change us. It should certainly purge our souls of all complacency.

As we roll up our sleeves and dig into the topic of hell, it's important that you don't distance what the Bible says from reality. In other words, don't forget that the *doctrine* you are studying may be the *destiny* of many people. Hell should not be studied without tearful prayer. We must weep, pray, and fast over this issue, begging God to reveal to us through His Word the truth about hell. Because we can't be wrong on this one.

## Let God Be God

But this book is actually much more than a book on hell. It's a book about embracing a God who isn't always easy to understand, and whose ways are far beyond us; a God whose thoughts are much higher than our thoughts; a God who, as the sovereign Creator and Sustainer of all things, has every right to do, as the psalmist says, "whatever He pleases" (Ps. 115:3 NASB).

God has the right to do WHATEVER He pleases.

If I've learned one thing from studying hell, it's that last line. And whether or not you end up agreeing with everything I say about hell, you must agree with Psalm 115:3. Because at the end of the day, our feelings and wants and heartaches and desires are not ultimate—only God is ultimate. God tells us plainly that His ways and thoughts are infinitely higher than ours (Isa. 55:9). Expect then, that Scripture will say things that don't agree with your natural way of thinking.

This is why we need to pray. We need to ask God to help us think rightly about hell. Before you read this book, I ask that you pray. Seriously. Pray. I'm the type of person who never does what a book tells me to do, and maybe you are too. But I ask you to make this one exception. Pray before you read this book. The following is the gist of the prayers I prayed as I journeyed along in the writing of this book. It's also my prayer for you as you wrestle with this important issue:

*God, I want to know what is true. I know I have cravings that sway and distort my ability to reason. You promise that Your Holy Spirit will guide me into all truth. I pray that He will now. I don't want to be wrong. I don't want to be deceived by others or myself. You alone possess all truth, and I want to be on Your side. Give me eyes to see and ears to hear. Give me courage to live and speak what is right no matter the cost. I don't want to believe anything about You that is not true. Amen.*

# Chapter 1

# Does Everyone Go to Heaven?

Does everyone go to heaven?

Based on what I hear at funerals, the answer is an overwhelming "Yes!" How many funerals have you attended where this was even in question?

What we need to do is get down to what the Bible says about the matter. Questions about heaven and hell are too important to leave to our feelings or assumptions. But before we examine the biblical answers to these things, we have to settle an important question.

Do you want to believe in a God who shows His power by punishing non-Christians and who magnifies His mercy by blessing Christians forever?

Do you *want* to? Be honest.

Do you *want* to believe in a God like this? Here's my gut-level, honest answer:

No.

No way. I have family and friends who reject Jesus. I do not *want* to believe in a God who punishes non-Christians. Okay, maybe He should punish extremely wicked people—that makes some sense. But punishment in hell for seemingly good people, or those who simply chose the wrong religion? That feels a bit harsh, at least according to my sense of justice.

But let me ask you another question. *Could* you?

*Could you* believe in a God who decides to punish people who don't believe in Jesus? A God who wants to show His power by punishing those who don't follow His Son?

Now that's a different question, isn't it? You may not recognize the difference immediately, but read them again and you'll see that these two questions—*do you want to?* versus *could you?*—are actually miles apart.

The problem is that we often respond to the second question *because of* our response to the first. In other words, because there are things that we don't *want* to believe about God, we therefore decide that we *can't* believe them.

Let me be more specific and personal. I *want* everyone to be saved. I do. I *don't want* anyone to go to hell. The fact is, I would love for all people to stand before Christ on judgment day and have a chance to say, "They were right all along, Jesus. You really are the Savior. I am so sorry for not believing in You before, but I believe now. Can I have a second chance?"

I *want* to believe in a God who will save everyone in the end.

But is this what God says He will do? Do the Scriptures teach this? Despite what we may *want* to believe, we've got to figure out what God told us to believe in His Word. That's what this chapter is all about. We're going to tackle the question: *Does the Bible say that everyone will be saved in the end?*

## Universalism: A Brief Survey

Throughout history, some Christians have not only wanted God to save everyone but have gone on to argue that the Bible says He will. This view is called Universalism.[1] The most famous proponent of Universalism was an early church leader named Origen (ca. AD 185–254), who seemed to teach this, though his views were very complex and not always consistent.[2] Origen's beliefs were later deemed heretical,[3] but this didn't stop others from embracing the view that everyone will be saved—though advocates were always a minority. In fact, for over 1,600 years, hardly any major theologians argued that everyone will be saved. This all began to change in the 1800s, when several thinkers resurrected Origen's beliefs and put them back on the table. Today, there are a growing number of confessing Christians who reflect in one way or another the views of Origen on matters of salvation and the afterlife. Even some evangelicals, such as Thomas Talbott and Gregory MacDonald, have argued that God will end up saving everyone in the end.[4]

Most recently, author Rob Bell finds this view compelling. With creativity and wit, he sets forth a similar position, though he avoids the label *Universalism*. Nevertheless, Bell suggests that every single person will embrace Jesus—if not in this life, then certainly in the next.[5] He writes:

> At the heart of this perspective is the belief that, given enough time, everybody will turn to God and find themselves in the joy and peace of God's presence. The love of God will melt every hard heart, and even the most "depraved sinners" will eventually give up their resistance and turn to God.[6]

It's important to understand that Universalism comes in many shapes and sizes. This is why we have to be careful about slapping the label *Universalist* on people who say that everyone will end up being saved. The term *Universalist* is about as specific as the term *Baptist*. If you call someone a Baptist, all you've said is that they don't baptize babies—beyond this, it's pretty much up for grabs. In the same way, all Universalists believe that everyone will end up being saved, but this belief is expressed in a variety of ways.

For instance, there are *non-Christian* Universalists. Sometimes called *Pluralists,* these people believe that Jesus is one of many ways to salvation. Pluralists believe that all religions present equally valid ways of salvation—Christianity is simply one among many.

Then there are *Christian* Universalists, some of whom call themselves *hopeful* Universalists. They believe that Christ is the only way, but they hold out hope that God will end up saving everyone through Christ in the end. But they go beyond simply *hoping* this will happen (don't we all?). They're hopeful, *and* they see strong biblical support for this view, though their view is often tempered with caution.

The least cautious *Christian* Universalists call themselves *dogmatic* Universalists. Like the previous group, they believe that Christ is the only way, but they go a bit further and say that the Bible clearly teaches that all will be saved. They find the view not just possible, but the most probable: They believe that the Bible clearly teaches that all will be saved through Jesus in the end.

It's important, then, to understand that *Christian* Universalists (hopeful and dogmatic) believe that salvation is by grace through faith in Christ and Christ alone. There's nothing untraditional about this. The difference is that they believe people will have another chance (or many chances) after death to believe in Jesus and be saved.

## Universalism in the Bible

But how do they arrive at these views? As attractive as this position is, does anything in the Bible support the idea that God will end up saving everyone?

Maybe. At first glance, some passages seem to support the notion that everyone will be saved. But after taking a closer look, it doesn't appear that they do. We don't have time or space to cover every passage used to support Christian Universalism, so we'll take a look at a few of the big ones: Philippians 2, 1 Corinthians 15, 1

Timothy 2, and Revelation 21. We'll then conclude by looking at what the Bible says about choosing Jesus after we die.

## Every Knee Will Bow

If you were on a deserted island and you uncorked an empty bottle containing Philippians 2:9–11, you would probably be a Universalist. After talking about Christ's humble life, death, and resurrection, Paul says:

> Therefore God has highly exalted him and
> bestowed on him the name that is above every
> name, so that at the name of Jesus every knee
> should bow, in heaven and on earth and under the
> earth, and every tongue confess that Jesus Christ is
> Lord, to the glory of God the Father.

The key phrase here is "every knee should bow … and every tongue confess that Jesus Christ is Lord" (vv. 10–11). By itself, this could mean that every single individual who ever lived will embrace Jesus—if not in this life, then surely in the next.

But all we would need is for the rest of the Philippian letter to float ashore in order to see that Philippians 2:9–11 doesn't teach universal salvation. In Philippians 1:28, Paul says that those who oppose the gospel will face "destruction," while those who embrace it will be saved. There's a contrast here between believers and unbelievers; each have very different destinies. In Philippians 3:19, Paul refers to the enemies of Christ whose "end is destruction," while followers of Jesus look forward to resurrection and glory (3:20–21). Once more, there's a contrast. A contrast between believers and unbelievers and their individual destinies (note the word *end* in 3:19), which follow the decisions they make in this life.

We also need to see that Paul in Philippians 2 is actually quoting from the Old Testament book of Isaiah. Here, the prophet Isaiah looks forward to a time when every knee will bow and every tongue will confess the name of God (45:23). But in that passage, Isaiah is referring to God's salvation, which is *witnessed* among the nations and embraced by *some* but not all. In fact, Isaiah himself, in the very passage that Paul quotes, says that there will be some who embrace salvation and some who continue to resist it.[7]

So what does Philippians 2:9–11 mean? It means that there will come a day when Christ returns to reclaim His creation, and *everyone will acknowledge this*. King Jesus will reign, and none will be able to deny it. But Paul doesn't contradict Isaiah.[8] With this salvation and reign also comes judgment for those who opposed Christ in this life. Isaiah said this in the very next verse (45:24), and Paul affirms it as well (Phil. 1:28; 3:19).

## All Will Be Made Alive

Several passages in the New Testament describe God restoring all people or reconciling all things to Himself. These verses are often used to prove that God will save every single person.[9] Here are a few of the big ones:

For as in Adam all die, so also in Christ shall all be made alive. (1 Cor. 15:22)

In Christ God was reconciling the world to himself, not counting their trespasses against them, and entrusting to us the message of reconciliation. (2 Cor. 5:19)

In him all the fullness of God was pleased to dwell, and through him to reconcile to himself all things, whether on earth or in heaven, making peace by the blood of his cross. (Col. 1:19–20)

[God] desires all people to be saved and to come to the knowledge of the truth. (1 Tim. 2:4)

In looking at these passages, one Christian Universalist says, "Paul envisioned a time when all persons would be reconciled to God in the full redemptive sense."[10]

Is that what these passages are saying, or is there something else going on?

There seems to be something else going on in 1 Corinthians 15:22, for instance, where Paul says, "In Christ all will be made alive" (NIV). The verse by itself could mean that everyone will end up being saved, but the context doesn't support this interpretation. When Paul says "all will be made alive," he's clearly thinking about the resurrection of *believers* at the second coming of Christ. In fact, he says this very thing in the next verse: "All who belong to Christ will be made alive at his coming" (see vv. 22–23).[11] So the verse can't mean that everyone will be saved in the end. In fact, following this verse is a whole lot of destruction: destruction of everyone and everything that opposes God in this life (vv. 25–26).[12] This is why Paul concludes the letter with a forceful warning that everyone who does not love Jesus will be damned (16:22).

So in this case, "all" doesn't mean every single person. And this is a good thing to keep in mind when looking at 1 Corinthians 15:22 and other passages like it. You've got to figure out from the context what "all" means. For instance, when Mark said that "*all* the country of Judea" and "*all* the people of Jerusalem" were going out to be baptized by John (Mark 1:5 NASB), he certainly didn't mean every single individual in Judea—man, woman, and child. "All" here simply denotes a large number of people. In Acts 21:28, Paul is accused of preaching to "all men everywhere" (NASB). Did Paul really share the gospel with every single person on earth? Again, "all" means a whole lot of people in many different places, not every single individual.

So "all" doesn't always mean everything or everyone. And the same goes for 1 Corinthians 15:22, as is clear from the context. The "all" who will be "made alive" in Christ refers to believers of all types, not every single person.

## Does God Get What God Wants?

The same goes for 1 Timothy 2:4, which says: God "wants all people to be saved" (TNIV).

We could spin a provocative question out of this verse by asking, *Does God get what God wants?*[13] And this would set up a rhetorical slam dunk. Of course God gets what He wants! Otherwise, He's not God. Or if He is God, He's not very powerful.

But hold on a second. This question of God getting what He wants passes over two other important questions about 1 Timothy 2:4: (1) What's the meaning of "all," and (2) what does the word *want* mean in this context?

The first question is fairly easy to answer in light of our discussion above. Once again, the context is key. Just a few verses earlier, Paul commands Timothy to pray for "all people" (1 Tim. 2:1), and this command is based on God's desire to save "all people" (v. 4). If we take the second "all people" to mean every single person, then surely we've got to take the other "all" in the same way. Does Paul really want us to march through a prayer list that includes every person on the face of the earth? Maybe this wouldn't be a bad thing, but I don't think this is Paul's point here. In 1 Timothy 2:1–2, he qualifies the prayer for "all people" by adding "for kings and all who are in high positions." It seems that Paul is urging Timothy to pray for all types of people—even those Roman leaders who may persecute Christians!

It's probably the case that Paul wants Timothy to *pray* for all types of people because God is on a mission to *save* all types of people.

What then does Paul mean by "want"? This issue is a bit more complicated, because this word can mean all sorts of different things. In any case, the word *want* does not have to mean that God wants something and is doing all He can to get it, in the same way that I want a coffee refill and simply walk up to the counter and get it. In fact, Paul, who said that God wants all people to be saved, also said that God "wants" all Christians to be sexually pure (1 Thess. 4:3).[14]

Ever met a Christian who was not sexually pure? Does this mean that God is not getting what God wants?

To figure out the meaning of "want," it's helpful to consider what theologians have called God's *moral* will and His *decreed* will. Some things may be part of God's desire for the world, and yet these desires can be resisted. God doesn't *desire* that people sin, but He allows it to happen because humans are moral agents who often make evil choices. God is not a puppet master who pulls everyone's strings to suit His will. That's why the Lord taught us to pray things like "your will be done, on earth as it is in heaven" (Matt. 6:10). God's desire—His *moral* will—is resisted.

And then there's God's *decreed* will. This refers to those things that God makes happen regardless of what humans decide. He sometimes uses our bad choices—our rebellion against His *moral* will—to carry out His *decreed* will. There's a difference, in other words, between God's *values that please Him* (moral will) and those *events that He causes to happen* (decreed will).[15]

Is this getting too heavy? Maybe an illustration will help. In Judges 14—16, we read about a loose cannon named Samson. Though he was mighty in warfare, his moral compass was significantly flawed, as seen in his love for ladies of the pagan sort. At the beginning of the story, Samson fell in love with a Philistine woman, which was against God's *moral will* (Judg. 3:1–6). And yet Judges 14:4 says that his love affair was "from the LORD." God was "seeking an opportunity against the Philistines," and so He used Samson's lust to oppose the Philistines. Samson's love for pagan women went against God's *moral* will, but became part of God's *decreed* will. Samson was free to go against God's *moral* will, yet God intervened to carry out His *decreed* will in using this situation to fight against the Philistines.

Now back to 1 Timothy 2. In what sense does God *want* all people to be saved? The word underscores God's *moral* will, His desire to save all types of people. They are free to reject this because it isn't God's decreed will, but the verse captures God's heart nonetheless. So a question framed as, *does God get what God wants?* implies that if He doesn't save everyone as He set out to, then He's a failure. But this is a naive assumption at best; at worst, the rhetoric is tremendously misleading.

Paul's point is *not* that Timothy is to pray for every single person who ever lived, and neither is it that God has decreed that He will save everyone. The point of 1 Timothy 2 and other passages like it (e.g., 2 Peter 3:9) is that God is not a bigot; He's not a racist; He loves to reverse social-class distinctions because His love knows no boundaries. The gospel has broken down all ethnic and socio-economic barriers through the cross of Jesus Christ, as Paul says elsewhere (Eph. 2:11–22).[16] God even wants pedophile maniacs like Caesar Nero (i.e., "kings and all who are in high positions" in 1 Tim. 2:2) to repent and come to Jesus! Paul nearly got to Nero with the gospel and had his head chopped off in the process. But that's another story.

## Who Left the Gate Open?

Let's flip to the last book of the Bible, where some argue that all will ultimately be saved. Revelation 21 envisions believers flowing into the "New Jerusalem," which in one way or another depicts our final state. John, the writer, says that "its gates will never be shut" (v. 25) and that "the kings of the earth" will "bring their glory into" the New Jerusalem (v. 24). But who left that gate open? What is John saying by using this image of open gates? Some have taken this to mean that God will forever wait with open arms (or open gates) for unbelievers to turn to Him. "Once they have been purified in the lake of fire," says one writer, "those most vile of all men … will be free to enter the New Jerusalem through gates that never close."[17]

But does the image of open gates show that "those who have said no to God's love in this life" will have endless opportunities to say yes to it in the afterlife?[18] This is an interesting suggestion. I would love to believe it, but three things in the text make it hard for me to accept that theory. First, Revelation 20 and 21 have already described the "lake of fire" as the final destiny of those who don't follow Jesus in this life. There's nothing in Revelation that suggests there's hope on the other side of the lake. Second, there's nothing in the text that says the lake of fire is intended to *purify* the wicked. On the contrary, the judgment scene in 20:11–15 explains that the lake of fire is for *punishment*.[19] And third, even after the open-gates passage of 21:24–26, John goes on to depict two different destinies for believers and unbelievers:

> Blessed are those who wash their robes, so that
> they may have the right to the tree of life and that
> they may enter the city by the gates. Outside are
> the dogs and sorcerers and the sexually immoral
> and murderers and idolaters, and everyone who
> loves and practices falsehood. (22:14–15)

This passage says that there will be an ongoing separation between believers and unbelievers. What determines their destinies is whether or not they "wash[ed] their robes;" in other words, whether or not their sin has been dealt with through the blood of Jesus in *this life* (see Rev. 7:14). I think it's a stretch to suggest that unbelievers can wash their robes while in the lake of fire and then enter the gates.

To sum it up, there are some passages in the New Testament that seem to say everyone will be saved. But after looking at the context, we see that these passages probably don't mean this. Not only would this contradict many other passages that speak of judgment and retribution (as we will see in the following chapters), it doesn't align well with the context of the passages themselves.

### What about Those Passages That Say There Will Be a Second Chance?

I said at the beginning that the one thing all Christian Universalists agree upon is that after death there will be another chance (or an endless string of chances) to choose Jesus. The Universalist view depends upon it. So we need to wrestle with all the postmortem second-chance passages to see if they actually teach this view. The problem is, there aren't any passages that say this.

No passage in the Bible says that there will be a second chance after death to turn to Jesus.

And that's frightening. It's frightening because the idea of an after-death conversion is the most important ingredient for the Universalist position. It makes or breaks this view. But there is no single passage in the Bible that describes, hints at, hopes for, or suggests that someone who dies without following Jesus in this life will have an opportunity to do so after death. One Christian Universalist admits this. Arguing for the possibility of people getting out of hell, he says:

> Clearly my interpretation is underdetermined by
> the texts.... I am not so much exegeting the texts
> as trying to draw out the logic of New Testament

theology as I understand it and its implications for
those texts. In the process I may be offering ways
of reading the texts that go beyond what their
authors had in mind.[20]

Keep in mind that we're not simply trying to settle a doctrinal
issue. We're talking about people's destinies. The thought that someone may end up banking on a second chance after they die even
though the biblical authors never explicitly said this is … well …
Terrifying.

These are eternal *destinies* we're talking about. We can't be wrong
on this one. To make a compelling case that "the love of God will
melt every hard heart, and even the most 'depraved sinners' will
eventually give up their resistance and turn to God"[21] without clear
biblical evidence is incredibly dangerous—especially if you are one
of these "sinners" and things don't work out like this. If the doctor
said your daughter is going to be fine, and she died three days later,
you'd call the authorities.

The Bible does not say that there will be a second chance after
death. In fact, some passages even warn against this type of false
hope.

For instance, toward the end of His life, Jesus told a parable
about second chances (Luke 13:22–30).[22] Jesus is making His way
to Jerusalem, and His disciples ask how many people will end up
being saved. Jesus answers that few will be saved, but even worse,
many who think they are saved will end up on the "outside" of the
kingdom, so to speak. While outside, they'll knock on the door to

see if Jesus will let them in. What will happen when Jesus comes to the door?

According to those who believe that there are second chances after death, Jesus answers, "Come on in!" He has to, right? To think that Jesus would answer any other way is cruel. It would be unloving and unjust! Could Jesus actually say, "'Door's locked. Sorry. If you had been here earlier, I could have done something. But now, it's too late'"?[23]

Yes, actually, He could. Though we may wish for the door to fling open, Jesus says that He will do the opposite:

> "When once the master of the house has risen
> and shut the door, and you begin to stand outside
> and to knock at the door, saying, 'Lord, open
> to us,' then he will answer you, 'I do not know
> where you come from.… Depart from me, all you
> workers of evil!' In that place there will be weeping
> and gnashing of teeth, when you see Abraham
> and Isaac and Jacob and all the prophets in the
> kingdom of God but you yourselves cast out."
> (Luke 13:25–28)

This passage "gives no hint whatever that the door will remain permanently open."[24] If Jesus believed in second chances for those who reject Him in this life, then this parable is dangerously misleading.

For those who follow Jesus, there is everlasting life in the presence of God, but for those who don't follow Him, there will be punishment. And as we have seen in this chapter, the Bible doesn't seem to hold out hope for a second chance.[25] How scary this is for those who will find themselves on the other side of the door wanting to come in, banging and begging, wishing they had made some different choices while they had the opportunity.

It's sobering to think about this parable. Jesus did not say these words so we would one day merely discuss them in a book. Like all Scripture, this parable is meant to impact our souls. Please take some time to at least read it again. Read it with care. Read it with conviction, knowing that there will be people on the outside, in a terrible place of punishment.

A place called hell.

# Notes

1.  For a historical survey, see Richard Bauckham, "Universalism—A Historical Survey," *Themelios* 4.2 (1979): 48–54; Morwenna Ludlow, "Universalism in the History of Christianity," in Robin A. Parry and Christopher H. Partridge, eds., *Universal Salvation? The Current Debate* (Grand Rapids, MI: Eerdmans, 2003): 191–218.

2.  For elaboration on the inconsistencies of Origen's thought, especially his views on universal salvation, see Mark S. M. Scott, "Guarding the Mysteries of Salvation: The Pastoral Pedagogy of Origen's Universalism," *Journal of Early Christian Studies* 18.3 (2010): 347–68; Tom Greggs, "Exclusivist or Universalist? Origen the 'Wise Steward of the Word' (*CommRom.* V.1.7) and the Issue of Genre," *International Journal of Systematic Theology* 9.3 (2007): 315–327.

3.  Origen's views were deemed heretical at the fifth ecumenical church council held at Constantinople in AD 553. However, a great deal of politics drove this council, as well as other early church councils, so we shouldn't consider Origen's views heretical based solely on the decisions made at Constantinople.

4.  Thomas Talbott, *The Inescapable Love of God* (Boca Raton, FL: Universal Publishers, 1999); Gregory MacDonald, *The Evangelical Universalist* (Eugene, OR: Cascade Books, 2006). Gregory MacDonald is a pseudonym.

5. In his book *Love Wins,* Bell never actually comes out and says that this is what he believes. To be fair, he is not explicitly arguing for this position but listing it as a valid view that would help explain a lot of the tension that we feel when thinking about the hard realities of hell. But he presents this position in such favorable terms that it would be hard to say that he is not advocating it. He even says the traditional view of a literal hell that features eternal torment is not "good news" at all. To use Bell's phrase, "The good news is better than that." He implies the view that all people will eventually be saved is actually much better news. So while he never says that this is the *correct* view, Bell certainly presents this view as the *good* view and the traditional view of hell as the *bad* view. See *Love Wins* (New York: HarperOne, 2011), 110–111, 173–175.

6. Bell, *Love Wins,* 107.

7. See Howard Marshall, "The New Testament Does Not Teach Universal Salvation," in Parry and Partridge, *Universal Salvation,* 68–69. This reading is supported by the conclusion of the book of Isaiah, which depicts two groups of people, those on God's side and those who remain against Him: "[A]ll flesh shall come to worship before me, declares the LORD. And they shall go out and look on the dead bodies of the men who have rebelled against me. For their worm shall not die, their fire shall not be quenched, and they shall be an abhorrence to all flesh" (66:23–24). And that's how Isaiah ends. There will be restoration for those who turn to God, and judgment followed by punishment for those who don't.

8.  Throughout Isaiah 40—66, the nations will "see" (40:5; 52:10, 15), "understand" (52:15) and even "know" about (45:6; 49:26) God's salvation of His people, but this doesn't mean that they embrace it. For instance, Isaiah says that the pagan king Cyrus the Great will "know that it is … the LORD" who raised him up, and yet the next verse says "though you do not *know* me" (Isa. 45:3–4). So does Cyrus "know" God or not? Yes and no. He *knows* God in the sense that he acknowledges God's sovereignty, but he doesn't *know* God so as to believe in Him for salvation.

    Now, to be sure, there will be many among the nations (i.e., Gentiles) who will embrace this God of Israel. This is an important theme in Isaiah as well (44:5; 45:14, 20– 25; 49:7; 55:5). But Isaiah never says that everyone without exception will be saved.

9.  Passages include Romans 5:18–19, Romans 11:32, and Ephesians 1:10.

10. Thomas Talbott, "Christ Victorious," in Parry and Partridge, *Universal Salvation*, 25. Similarly, Rob Bell says "no one can resist God's pursuit forever, because God's love will eventually melt even the hardest of hearts" (*Love Wins*, 108). In this quote, Bell is thinking of Colossians 1 in particular.

11. I've switched the order of words in 15:22–23 for clarity, but the meaning I'm giving here is clear from the context.

12. Thomas Talbott claims that God will only destroy the sinful nature of unbelievers, according to this passage ("Christ

Victorious," 27). But there's nothing in the actual text to justify this interpretation.

13. This is the title of chapter 4 in Bell's *Love Wins*.

14. First Thessalonians 4:3 says "For this is the will of God, your sanctification: that you abstain from sexual immorality." The Greek word for "will" is *thelema*, which is the noun form of the verb translated "want" in 1 Timothy 2:4 (NIV).

15. See Millard Erickson, *Christian Theology*, 2nd ed. (Grand Rapids, MI: Baker, 1998), 387–88. Of course, it may be that God's decreed will includes the very resistance of His moral will. But that's getting a bit off track.

16. N. T. Wright calls this "biblical universalism" in his "Towards a Biblical View of Universalism," *Themelios* 4.2 (1979): 54–58.

17. Thomas Talbott, "A Pauline Interpretation of Divine Judgment," in Parry and Partridge, *Universal Salvation*, 42. See also Vernard Eller, *The Most Revealing Book of the Bible: Making Sense Out of Revelation* (Grand Rapids, MI: Eerdmans, 1974), 200–201; Bell, *Love Wins*, 114–115.

18. As Bell suggests (*Love Wins*, 114–115).

19. More specifically, retributive punishment and not remedial punishment.

20. MacDonald, *The Evangelical Universalist,* 140.

21. Bell, *Love Wins,* 107.

22. The parable is not exclusively about the afterlife, because "the kingdom" is a present reality. However, the parable certainly includes the afterlife, because the kingdom extends into the age to come. Moreover, Jesus' words "in that place there will be weeping and gnashing of teeth" (13:28), along with people being "cast out" (13:28) clearly point to hell, as they do elsewhere in Matthew (see 8:12; 22:13; 25:30). See Marshall, "The New Testament Does Not Teach Universal Salvation," 59.

23. The quote is from Bell, who raises this question in *Love Wins,* 108. In the context, Bell is summarizing the view that he finds legitimate and compelling, though he doesn't necessarily say it's correct.

24. Marshall, "The New Testament Does Not Teach Universal Salvation," 59.

25. See also Matthew 25:1–12; Hebrews 9:27; Revelation 22:11.

# Chapter 2

## Has Hell Changed? Or Have We?

I am embarrassed to admit this, but when I hear the name *Jesus,* a picture often appears in my mind. It's a painting of a Caucasian male with long blond hair, staring into the sky. It hung on the wall of a church I once attended. Growing up, I saw it every Sunday morning. It bothers me now, because it is ridiculously inaccurate. I know that Jesus did not look that way when He walked the earth, and He certainly doesn't look like that now. But as hard as I have tried, I have not been able to erase that picture from my memory. It occasionally creeps back into my mind when I hear the name *Jesus.* Sometimes it even happens when I'm praying! I doubt anyone struggled with this problem two thousand years ago.

Today, when you say the name *Jesus,* all sorts of images appear in our minds. There are millions of different ideas about what He was and is like. Some people, like me, have inaccurate images that we are still trying to shake. Others create new ideas about Jesus and spend their lives trying to convince themselves those ideas are true. Deep down, we all have a tendency to recreate Jesus in our own image. Before we know it, we have an American Jesus, a Western Jesus, a postmodern Jesus, a hippie Jesus, or a capitalistic or socialistic Jesus. Deep down in the heart of every person is a hidden desire to reinterpret Jesus in light of our own culture, political bent, or favorite theological belief.

We do the same thing with hell. The question "what is hell?" has spawned many answers over the years. For Origen, hell was a place where the souls of the wicked were purified so they could find their way back to God. Dante depicted hell as a place under the earth's surface with nine levels of suffering, where sinners were bitten by snakes, tormented by beasts, showered with icy rain, and trapped in rivers of blood or flaming tombs; some were even steeped in huge pools of human excrement. C. S. Lewis's portrayal of hell was significantly less creepy. For Lewis, it was kind of like a dark, gloomy city, or a place where "being fades away into nonentity."[1] A happier portrait of hell was painted by the band AC/DC, who said that "hell ain't a bad place to be"—it's where all our friends are.[2] Most recently, Rob Bell said that hell is not "about someday, somewhere else,"[3] but about the various "hells on earth" that people experience in this life—genocide, rape, and unjust socioeconomic structures.[4]

Through the years, many ideas of hell have been proposed—some attractive, some not. But if truth is what we are after, we need to stick to what Jesus actually said. We also need to try to understand Jesus' statements in the context of the world He lived in. We need to enter Jesus' world, His first-century *Jewish* world, if we're going to figure out what He meant when He spoke of hell.

We need to enter Jesus' world because Jesus was a Jew, a Jew who lived two thousand years ago in the Middle East. He spoke Aramaic and also a bit of Greek, though probably with an accent. He didn't know a lick of English—certainly nothing of the Elizabethan, KJV sort. He was a blue-collar man who worked long hard days as a woodworker (or mason), and probably bore the physical features of a hardworking peasant: dark leathery skin, calloused hands, and a few scars here and there from working in the shop. Jesus probably didn't have long hair because this wasn't typical of Jewish men of His day, and He certainly didn't have blue eyes, blond hair, and milky white skin.

Jesus was a first-century Jew, so we need to leave behind all our Jesuses that have been refashioned and reshaped by our own cultural biases. The only way we're going to understand what Jesus said about hell is to soak ourselves in the Bible's own culture. Breathe its air. Feel its dirt. Smell the scent of first-century Palestine—and *then* we'll be in a better position to understand more clearly what Jesus and His followers were saying about hell.

So to this world we turn. What we find in this context is that hell was seen as a place of punishment for those who don't follow God. In fact, so ingrained was the belief in hell among first-century Jews[5] that Jesus would have had to go out of His way to distance Himself from these beliefs if He didn't hold them. In the next chapter, we'll consider whether or not Jesus actually does this. For now, we'll dig into the Jewish culture around Him to see what His contemporaries said about hell.

Specifically, in this chapter we'll see that for the Jews of Jesus' day:

1. Hell is a place of punishment after judgment.
2. Hell is described in imagery of fire and darkness, where people lament.
3. Hell is a place of annihilation or never-ending punishment.

So let's take a quick tour of some of these Jewish writers to see what they say about hell.[6] Just to be clear, none of the passages we'll look at here are in the New Testament; rather, they were written by Jews right around the same time (200 BC—AD 100). To keep it simple, I'll just reference the dates of passages throughout and leave the rest of the information for the notes. I realize that some of you reading this are not on the edge of your seats thinking, *Cool! I love studying first-century Judaism!* But try to stay with me. I think a short history lesson is necessary to help us erase any twenty-first century ideas of Jesus we may have added.

## The First-Century Jewish View of Hell

Jews in the first century used the Old Testament to build their theology. But the Old Testament doesn't say much about hell. The doctrine of hell is progressively developed throughout Scripture, much like heaven, the Holy Spirit, and even Jesus. This definitely does *not* mean that these things changed over time; God simply reveals more and more about them as Scripture unfolds. We see this especially with hell. The Old Testament does make a few vague references to punishment in the afterlife; Daniel 12:2 is the most relevant: "Many of those who sleep in the dust of the earth shall awake, some to everlasting life, and *some to shame and everlasting contempt*" (see also Ezek. 32:17–32). Such statements, though, are infrequent in the Old Testament. It's not until the New Testament that these ideas are fully revealed.

Many first-century Jews, while studying the Old Testament (Daniel 12 in particular), developed certain beliefs about hell. Again, these beliefs are not in themselves inspired by God. Understand that I am not attempting in this chapter to determine whether or not the conclusions of first-century Jews were accurate. I am just describing the common beliefs about hell that Jesus and other New Testament writers would have grown up with. In general, here's what the first-century Jews believed.

## Hell Is a Place of Punishment after Judgment

The typical afterlife scenario among Jews in Jesus' day was that after the wicked die, they go to a place called hades, sometimes called sheol. This is not the same thing as "hell." Hades is not usually depicted as a place of punishment, though the wicked may suffer there. It is a place where the wicked wait until judgment day. After they are judged, the wicked are then thrown into hell as punishment for their sins. It's important to note that for the first-century Jew, this punishment is not *corrective* or *remedial* (think "remedy"); in other words punishment doesn't make them fit for salvation. Rather, hell is *retributive*—it's God's punishment for sin. Consider the following:

> [T]he chambers shall give up the souls which have
> been committed to them. And the Most High
> shall be revealed upon the seat of judgment ...
> recompense shall follow ... unrighteous deeds shall
> not sleep. Then the pit of torment shall appear
> ... and the furnace of Gehenna shall be disclosed.
> (first century AD)[7]

The same writer described gehenna, or hell, as a place of "fire and torments," where the wicked "wander about in torments, ever grieving and sad." Worst of all, this judgment is final, "because they cannot now make a good repentance that they may live."[8]

According to another Jewish writer,

> [T]he sinners are set apart when they die and are
> buried in the earth and judgment has not been
> executed upon them in their lifetime, upon this
> great pain, until the great day of judgment—and
> to those who curse (there will be) plague and pain
> forever, and the retribution of their spirits. (second
> century BC)[9]

Here, after sinners die they go to a place where they await judgment. The author even notes that they have *not* received judgment in their lifetime. In other words, hell is not considered to be the various "hells on earth" that we face every day. It's a horrific place of judgment where God punishes people for their sins.[10]

## Hell Is Described in Images of Fire, Darkness, and Lament

Of all the images used to describe hell, fire is the most common. Consider the following:

> [T]he coming world will be given to these [i.e., the ones obedient to God], but the habitation of the many others will be in *fire*. (first century AD)[11]

> Woe unto you, sinners, because of the works of your hands! On account of the deeds of your wicked ones, in *blazing flames worse than fire*, it shall burn. (first century BC)[12]

On judgment day, all the sinners whose names are "blotted out of the book of life" will "cry and lament in a place that is an invisible wilderness and *burn in the fire*." This place "was *completely dark*" and yet "the *flame of its fire* … was burning brightly" (first century AD).[13] Hell is an "abyss … full of fire" where the wicked are "cast into this fiery abyss, and they were burned."[14]

Fire, darkness, lamenting. These are the typical images used by first-century Jews to describe hell, and, as we'll see, they are the same images used by Jesus and other New Testament writers.

Now, as for the duration of hell, there was difference of opinion among the Jews. Some believed that the wicked would be annihilated in hell (their personal existence would cease), while others believed the wicked would be punished forever in an ongoing state of torment.

## Hell Is a Place of Annihilation

Some Jewish writers believed that the wicked would be annihilated. One , who lived in Israel around the time of Jesus, put it like this:

> And their dwelling place will be in darkness and the
> place of destruction; and they will not die but melt
> away until I remember the world and renew the
> earth. And then they will die and not live, and their
> life will be taken away from the number of all men.
> (first century AD)[15]

The fact that they don't die right away but "melt away" suggests some period of suffering. But ultimately, for this Jewish writer, there will be an annihilation of the wicked.

## Hell Is a Place of Never-Ending Punishment

While some believed that the wicked would be annihilated, others believed that hell is a place of never-ending punishment. These Jewish writers described hell as a place of "all kinds of torture and torment" where "dark and merciless" beings would use "instruments of atrocities torturing without pity" (first to second century AD).[16] Hell was called an "abyss" where its "prisoners were in pain, looking forward to endless punishment" (first to second century AD).[17] Another writer described the wicked in hell:

> pleading that he may give them a little breathing
> spell from the angels of his punishment …
> begging for a little rest but find it not…. Light has
> vanished from before us and darkness has become
> your habitation forever and ever; because we have
> formerly neither had faith nor glorified the name
> of the Lord of the Spirits. (first century AD)[18]

One graphic account depicts seven brothers being martyred by some Greek overlords. After the first six die, the seventh brother, after being tortured, blurts out before he dies,

> Because of this, justice has laid up for you
> intense and eternal fire and tortures, and these

throughout all time will never let you go. (first century AD)[19]

He basically tells his torturer to go to hell.

We could go on and on, citing Jewish writer after Jewish writer, all living and writing around the time of Jesus. If you want even more references to hell from first-century Judaism, you can check out the notes.[20] But from the passages cited above, one thing is clear: First-century Jews believed in hell. While there's some difference of opinion regarding the duration of hell, its existence as a place of punishment that awaits the wicked was nearly unanimously held.[21] This is undeniable. This is the first-century *Jewish* view of hell.[22]

And this Jewish world is the one Jesus grew up in. If we want to understand Jesus in light of His own first-century context, then we need to understand what this context believed about hell. This will keep us from reading back into the New Testament our own ideas about what Jesus was saying about hell.

## Is Hell a Garbage Dump?

Now, some recent writers do try to situate Jesus in His own context. This is actually one of the most encouraging aspects of Rob Bell's preaching and writing. Bell rightly says that to "grab a few lines of Jesus and drop them down on someone 2,000 years later without first entering into the world in which they first appeared is lethal to the life and vitality and *truth* of the Bible."[23] It's not just wrong, but "lethal to the ... *truth* of the Bible," says Rob. Amen!

In following Bell's advice, we have entered the world in which Jesus' statements on hell first appeared and have seen that this world believed in hell as a literal place of punishment. Bell also attempts to understand Jesus' view of hell in light of first-century Judaism but comes up with some very different results. We've already noted that Bell emphasizes that hell is the "hells on earth," the tragedies that this life brings, as opposed to a place of punishment for the wicked after death.[24] But this emphasis does not match the first-century scene, as you have seen firsthand.

Bell suggests that when Jesus used the word *hell* (gehenna), He referred to a garbage dump outside Jerusalem, where the Jews used to throw their trash. Bell argues that "Gehenna, in Jesus's day, was the city dump" and that this is what Jesus meant by hell:

> People tossed their garbage and waste into
> this valley. There was a fire there, burning
> constantly to consume the trash. Wild animals
> fought over the scraps of food along the edges
> of the heap. When they fought, their teeth
> would make a gnashing sound. Gehenna was
> the place with the gnashing of teeth, where the
> fire never went out. Gehenna was an actual

place that Jesus's listeners would have been
familiar with. So the next time someone asks
you if you believe in an actual hell, you can
always say, "Yes, I do believe that my garbage goes
somewhere …"[25]

But if Jesus was really referring to the literal city dump when He
spoke of gehenna, then many of His statements are awkward to say
the least:

"Whoever says, 'You fool!' will be liable to the
*garbage dump* of fire." (Matt. 5:22)

"It is better that you lose one of your members
than that your whole body be thrown into the
*garbage dump*." (Matt. 5:29)

"Fear him who can destroy both soul and body in
the *garbage dump*." (Matt. 10:28)

"It is better for you to enter life with one eye than
with two eyes to be thrown into the *garbage dump*
of fire." (Matt. 18:9)

Also, Jesus tells the scribes and Pharisees that they have made themselves "twice as much a child of the *garbage dump*" and then He asks, "How will you escape being condemned to the *garbage dump?*" (Matt. 23:15, 33, adapted).

While I applaud Bell's attempt to understand Jesus in His first-century Jewish context, his "gehenna is a garbage dump" theory is both misleading and inaccurate. Here's why.

First, it's misleading because it confuses the source of an idea for the idea itself.[26] Just because Jesus' description of hell may have been *inspired* by the image of a burning garbage dump (if it was) doesn't mean that He is referring to the actual garbage dump when He uses the word *gehenna*. For example, I've often heard people refer to a gridlocked freeway as a parking lot. The statement is inspired by a literal parking lot, but nobody is claiming that people drive to the freeway, stop, lock their cars, and then go about their business. That's just the way imagery works. So to say that Jesus was referring to an actual dump is to misunderstand the way language functions.

Second, the "gehenna is a garbage dump" suggestion is also inaccurate. The whole theory actually stands on very shaky evidence. Some commentaries and pastors still promote the idea, but there's no evidence from the time of Jesus that the Hinnom Valley (gehenna literally means "Valley of Hinnom") was the town dump. In fact, there is no evidence for hundreds and hundreds of years after Jesus that there ever was a garbage dump in the Hinnom Valley in the first century. Nor is there any archaeological evidence that this valley was ever a dump[27] (if it was a dump, we'd be able to dig around and find evidence). In fact, the first reference we have to the Hinnom Valley, or gehenna, as a town dump is made by a rabbi named David Kimhi in a commentary, which was written in AD 1200.

AD 1200! That's over a thousand years after Jesus lived! This is the first time that the Hinnom Valley was ever associated with the town dump. Here's the quote from Kimhi:

> Gehenna is a repugnant place, into which filth and cadavers are thrown, and in which fires perpetually burn in order to consume the filth and bones; on which account, by analogy, the judgment of the wicked is called "Gehenna."[28]

Kimhi, writing in the late Middle Ages—from Europe, by the way, not Israel—is the first one to make this suggestion. So here's the problem: What are the chances that Jesus is thinking of this town dump in using the term *gehenna* when we have no evidence that there was such a place until over a thousand years after He lived? There's no evidence in the piles and piles of Jewish and Christian writings preceding the time of Kimhi that the word *gehenna* was derived from the burning garbage in the Hinnom Valley.

And did you notice what Kimhi himself said about the word *gehenna?* He said that the garbage dump of "gehenna" became an "analogy" for "the judgment of the wicked." So, even the first writer to connect gehenna with the garbage dump saw it as an *analogy for the place where the wicked will be judged.*

Much of what Bell says about hell relies upon a legend from the Middle Ages.

So what was it about the Hinnom Valley that forged the word *gehenna* into an image of fiery judgment? In the Old Testament, the Hinnom Valley was the place where some Israelites engaged in idolatrous worship of the Canaanite gods Molech and Baal. It was here, in fact, where they sacrificed their children to these gods (2 Kings 16:3; 21:6) making them "pass through the fire" (Ezek. 16:20–21 NASB). When Jeremiah began to preach, the Hinnom Valley started to take on a metaphorical reference for the place where the bodies of the wicked would be cast (Jer. 7:29–34; 19:6–9; 32:35): "Behold, the days are coming … when it will no more be called … the Valley of the Son of Hinnom, but the Valley of Slaughter" (Jer. 7:32). Jews living between the Testaments picked up on this metaphor and ran with it. The word *gehenna* was widely used by Jews during the time of Jesus to refer to the fiery place of judgment for the wicked in the end times, as we have seen.[29]

For first-century Jews, the violent image of evildoers being punished in the Hinnom Valley provided a fitting analogy for God punishing the wicked in hell. Because Jesus lived and taught in this setting, His unqualified references to gehenna would have been taken to mean the same thing, unless He specified that He had something else in mind—a question that we will explore in the next chapter.

Understanding first-century Judaism and what those Jews believed about hell prepares us for understanding Jesus' teaching on the subject in His own context. As we turn to the next chapter, we need to ask ourselves a very important question: *Did Jesus affirm or reject this widespread first-century belief in hell?*

## Notes

1.  C. S. Lewis, *The Problem of Pain* (San Francisco: HarperOne, 1940), 129.

2.  AC/DC, "Hell Ain't a Bad Place to Be," *Let There Be Rock* © 1977 Atlantic Records.

3.  Bell, *Love Wins*, 81.

4.  For Rob Bell, hell is primarily the various hells on earth; at least this is the impression he gives in his book *Love Wins*. Hell is the evil of a child being molested by a family member (p. 72). Hell is the aftermath of the Rwandan genocide (pp. 70–71). Hell is "the very real experiences and consequences of rejecting our God-given goodness and humanity" (p. 73). It is important for Bell that we "don't take Jesus's very real and prescient warnings about judgment out of context, making them about someday, somewhere else" (p. 81). And the best word to capture all the "terrible evil that comes from the secrets hidden deep within our hearts all the way to the massive, society-wide collapse and chaos that comes when we fail to live in God's world God's way" is the word *hell* (p. 93). Now, in passing, Bell does say "there is hell later" along with a hell now (p. 79). And when he wrestles with the parable of the rich man and Lazarus (Luke 16), he mentions that the rich man is in "profound torment" (p. 77)—though he defines this torment as "living with the realities of not dying

to" the unjust socioeconomic system in his previous life. But other than these two side comments, virtually everything Bell says about hell refers to the various hells on earth, the evil of this world: rape, addictions, child abuse, poverty, violence, and so on. A similar view is taken by Andrew Perriman, *The Coming of the Son of Man: New Testament Eschatology for an Emerging Church* (Milton Keynes, UK: Paternoster, 2005), 74–97.

5.  Throughout this chapter, I'll be using the term *first century* broadly to refer to the general time of Jesus.

6.  This chapter is going to dig into the wild and complicated world of Second Temple Judaism. Throughout this chapter, I'll be using the translations and dates of the Jewish literature from James H. Charlesworth, ed., *The Old Testament Pseudepigrapha*, 2 vols. (New York: Doubleday: 1983, 1985). For the translations of the Apocrypha, I'm using the New Revised Standard Version; and for the Dead Sea Scrolls, Florentino Garcia-Martinez and Eibert Tigchelaar, eds., *The Dead Sea Scrolls Study Edition, 2 vols.* (Leiden, The Netherlands: Brill, 1997). There is a ton of secondary literature on the subject of early Jewish views of hell and the afterlife. Among the most helpful are Duane F. Watson, "Gehenna," in David Noel Freedman, ed., *The Anchor Bible Dictionary* (New York: Doubleday, 1992): 2.296–298, and Richard Bauckham, "Early Jewish Visions of Hell," *Journal of Theological Studies* 41 (1990): 355–85.

7.  *4 Ezra* 7:32–36.

8.  *4 Ezra* 7:38, 80, 82.

9.  *1 En.* 22:10–13.

10. See also *1 En.* 27:2–3: "This accursed valley is for those accursed forever; here will gather together all (those) accursed ones, those who speak with their mouth unbecoming words against the Lord.… Here they shall be gathered together, and here shall be their judgment, in the last days" (second century BC). For hell as a place of retribution, see *2 Bar.* 30:4–5; 54:21.

11. *2 Bar.* 44:15; see too *T. Zeb.* 10:3.

12. *1 En.* 100:9. See too *L.A.B.* 23:6: "[Hell is] the place of *fire* where the deeds of those doing wickedness against [God] will be expiated" (first century AD); *2 En.* 10:2 [J]: "And there is no light there, and a *black fire* blazes up perpetually, with a *river of fire* that comes out over the whole place" (first century AD).

13. *1 En.* 108:3–4. Another writer uses the imagery of fire and darkness together in *1 En.* 103:5–8. One writer even uses the image of worms and fire together, much as Jesus and Isaiah did (Isa. 66:24; Mark 9:48): "Woe to the nations that rise up against my people! The Lord Almighty will take vengeance on them in the day of judgment; he will send *fire and worms* into their flesh; they shall weep in pain forever" (Judith 16:17; first century BC).

14. *1 En.* 90:26–27; see also *2 En.* 40:13.

15. *L.A.B.* 16:3; see also Wis. 4:14–15; 1 QS 4:11–14; *1 En.* 91:9–14.

16. *2 En.* 10:1, 3 [J]. I'm following the first-century date for *2 Enoch* given in Charlesworth (ed.), but other scholars date this work in the second or third century AD. For similar references, see *1 En.* 53:3; 56:1; 62:11; 63:1, where these punishments seem to be *awaiting* the wicked after judgment, rather than happening upon death.

17. *2 En.* 40:13 [J].

18. *1 En.* 63:1–7.

19. 4 Macc. 12:12.

20. Hell is described as "the measure of fire, the depths of the abyss … the abundance of long-suffering, the truth of judgment … the mouth of hell, the standing place of vengeance … the picture of the coming punishment" and "the powers of the flame" (*2 Bar.* 59:5–12). On judgment day, God will "drag Beliar [the Devil], and his hosts also, into Gehenna," and He will then resurrect the dead and "cause fire" to "consume all the impious, and they will become as if they had not been created" (*Ascen. Is.* 4:14–18).

21. The Sadducees, who didn't believe in an afterlife, certainly wouldn't have believed in hell.

22. While some believed that upon death the wicked *awaited* punishment (as stated above), others believed that the wicked would enter fiery punishment immediately upon death. It seems that the Pharisees believed this. They said that the righteous receive rewards and the wicked receive punishment immediately after they die (*Ant.* 18.14). This also seems to be reflected in Jesus' parable of the rich man and Lazarus in Luke 16:19–31, which Richard Bauckham says is the only place in the New Testament that mentions punishment immediately upon death ("Early Jewish Visions of Hell," 376).

23. Rob Bell, *Velvet Elvis: Repainting the Christian Faith* (Grand Rapids, MI: Zondervan, 2005), 63.

24. At times, Bell does say that the behavior of the wicked will be corrected in the end (see *Love Wins,* 91–93). I assume that he's talking about hell as a place of correction in these contexts, though he doesn't use the term *hell.*

25. Ibid., 68. See also Perriman, *The Coming of the Son of Man,* 92: "By the first century, the Valley of Hinnom (in Greek *geenna,* gehenna) … had become the city's refuse dump, where slow fires smoldered day and night."

26. In linguistic terms, Bell confuses the *referent* with the *sense.* See D. A. Carson, *Exegetical Fallacies, 2nd ed.* (Grand Rapids, MI: Baker, 1996), 63–64.

27. See Lloyd R. Bailey, "Gehenna: The Topography of Hell," *Biblical Archaeologist* 49.3 (1986): 187–91.

28. Cited in Bailey, "Gehenna," 188. Some scholars still refer to this myth, but cite no evidence (see e.g., Perriman, *The Coming of the Son of Man*, 92–93). R. T. France mentions it but is doubtful regarding its veracity, citing Bailey's article (*The Gospel of Matthew* [New International Commentary on the New Testament] [Grand Rapids, MI: Eerdmans, 2007], 202). Others, like Bailey, dismiss the myth altogether (see G. R. Beasley-Murray, *Jesus and the Kingdom of God* [Grand Rapids, MI: Eerdmans, 1986], 376; Peter Head, "The Duration of Divine Judgment in the New Testament," in Kent Brower and Mark Elliott, eds., *Eschatology in Bible and Theology* [Downers Grove, IL.: Inter-Varsity Press, 1997], 223). Several bloggers also pointed this out shortly after *Love Wins* came out (see bibleplaces.org; et al.).

29. On gehenna, see Freedman, *The Anchor Bible Dictionary*, 2.296–298. For early Jewish references to gehenna as the place of punishment for the wicked, see *1 En.* 26–27; 54:1–6; 56:1–4; 90:24–27; *4 Ezra* 7:26–38; *Ascen. Is.* 4:14–18; *Sib. Or.* 4.179–91.

# Chapter 3

# What Jesus Actually Said about Hell

As I write this chapter about hell, I'm sitting in the middle of a busy Starbucks. Every time I look up from my computer screen, I see that I'm surrounded by thirsty customers racing to the counter to fuel up on lattes and iced teas and mochas. They're happy, busy, enjoying life, laughing, chatting, and, of course, texting. Two moms look as if they just got done jogging and sit next to me, digging into each other's lives. Another couple just left. They were all over each other—a typical young couple without a care in the world. The girl last in line looks sad. *Really sad.* It makes me wonder what just happened in her life. And what about the employees? Are they happy? Some look that way, but others don't.

Joy, laughter, coffee, jazz, texting, talking, flirting, friendship, depression and the hope to be freed from it one day. This is life! I love it—and so do they.

The place buzzes with life. Meanwhile, I sit here reading passage after passage after passage, which all say that *some of these people are going to hell*. It sickens me to say that, and I can't explain how conflicted I feel right now. There are at least a dozen people within ten feet of me right here, right now, that may end up in the agony that I'm studying. What do I do? Do I keep writing? Keep studying? Should I bag this whole book thing and start building relationships with them? How can I believe these passages yet sit here silently? I know that some of you have faced this same conflict. Even as you're reading this, there are probably people within a few feet of you who may also go to hell. What will you do? It could be that the Lord wants you to put the book down.

Coming face-to-face with these passages on hell and asking these tough questions is a heart-wrenching process.

It forces me back to a sobering reality: This is not just about doctrine; it's about destinies. And if you're reading this book and wrestling with what the Bible says about hell, you cannot let this be a mere academic exercise. You must let Jesus' very real teaching on hell sober you up. You must let Jesus' words reconfigure the way you live, the way you talk, and the way you see the world and the people around you.


## Jesus on Hell


In the last chapter, we took a tour of Jesus' world and saw that, without a doubt, first-century Jews believed in hell. They believed that hell was a place of punishment for the wicked after they faced God's judgment. They used various images to describe this hell, such as fire, darkness, and lamentation. Some Jews believed that the wicked would be annihilated after being cast into hell, while others described hell as a place of never-ending torment.

Now, in walks a Jewish rabbi named Yeshua, or Jesus. Based on everything we know about Jesus, we would expect Him to address the concept of the afterlife with much more compassion. Right? We can think of the Pharisees, who seem to have taken every opportunity to make the Old Testament Law as harsh as possible. A significant portion of Jesus' teaching was dedicated to freeing people from the impossible yoke of the Pharisees. Surely Jesus backed away from these terrifying images and emphasized the love of God when talking about the judgment day. Right?

Well, not exactly. In fact, not at all.

Jesus grew up in the world of beliefs described in the last chapter. He would be expected to believe the same stuff about hell that most Jews did. And if He didn't—if Jesus rejected the widespread Jewish belief in hell—then He would certainly need to be clear about this.

That last line is very important. Better read it again.

In other words, if Jesus did not agree with the view of hell presented in the last chapter, then He would have had to deliberately and clearly argue *against* it. Remember that Jesus certainly wasn't afraid of going against some commonly held Jewish ideas, such as their view of divorce (Matt. 5:32; 19:9), forgiveness (Matt. 18:21–22), wealth (Luke 18—19), and laws about the Sabbath (Mark 3:1–6). So we can be sure that if Jesus didn't challenge the Jewish view of hell, it wasn't because He was afraid to.

So let's pull the focus in from Jesus' world to what Jesus Himself actually said about hell. What we're going to see is that His views stand in line with the dominant first-century Jewish view of hell. To show this, we'll look at Jesus' words through the same categories used in the last chapter. For Jesus:

1. Hell is a place of punishment after judgment.
2. Hell is described in imagery of fire and darkness, where people lament.
3. Hell is a place of annihilation or never-ending punishment.

## Hell Is a Place of Punishment after Judgment

Jesus uses the word *gehenna* (translated as "hell") twelve times in the Gospels. He also uses images of fire and darkness in contexts where punishment after judgment is in view. A quick look at these statements shows that Jesus believed, like His Jewish contemporaries, that a horrific place of punishment awaits the wicked on judgment day.

The clearest example is Matthew 25:31–46, the longest and most detailed account of judgment day in the four gospels. Jesus begins by saying:

> "When the Son of Man comes in his glory, and
> all the angels with him, then he will sit on his
> glorious throne. Before him will be gathered all

> the nations, and he will separate people one from
> another as a shepherd separates the sheep from the
> goats." (vv. 31–32)

We'll take a detailed look at this passage toward the end of this chapter. For now, it's important to note that the event is judgment day, which will occur when Christ comes back. After Jesus looks at the evidence (vv. 33–45), He gives His verdict: Believers are awarded everlasting life, while unbelievers are awarded everlasting punishment. Though the *word* hell (gehenna) is not used here, the *concept* of hell is conveyed by the phrases "everlasting fire" (v. 41) and "everlasting punishment" (v. 46).[1]

Another place where the word *hell* is used in the context of judgment is Matthew 5. The whole passage talks about the potentially devastating outcome of going to an earthly court. But Jesus goes on to say that God's courtroom will be much worse, for here the Judge has the power to sentence you to the "hell [gehenna] of fire" (Matt. 5:22). This is not a vague reference to hell and certainly not a reference to a garbage dump. The legal context of this statement ensures that Jesus is referring to the consequences of judgment day.

Here's one more passage where gehenna is used in the context of God's future judgment:

> "You serpents, you brood of vipers, how are you to
> escape being sentenced to hell [gehenna]?" (Matt.
> 23:33)

The phrase *sentenced to hell* is once again reminiscent of something you would hear in a courtroom. Hell, as we have seen, is assigned to the wicked (in this case, the scribes and Pharisees) as a place of punishment. Jesus is not using the word *hell* to describe "the very real experiences and consequences of rejecting our God-given goodness and humanity."[2] Yes, a life of sin will certainly lead to some terrible life-experiences—lust destroys relationships, anger leads to violence, and covetousness leads to divorce. No doubt. But that's not what Jesus is talking about here. When Jesus uses stock phrases like "gehenna of fire" in legal contexts like this one, He means a literal place of punishment after judgment. He means hell.

## Hell Is Described in Imagery of Fire and Darkness

Like His Jewish contemporaries, Jesus often used the image of fire to describe hell. Here are a couple of examples from Matthew 13. As Jesus tells a parable about "wheat" and "weeds," He says:

> "Let both grow together until the harvest, and at
> the harvest time I will tell the reapers, Gather the
> weeds first and bind them in bundles to be burned,
> but gather the wheat into my barn." (v. 30)

By itself, this verse says very little, but Jesus goes on to explain the parable and clarifies what He means by the burning weeds:

"Just as the weeds are gathered and burned with fire, so will it be at the close of the age. The Son of Man will send his angels, and they will gather out of his kingdom all causes of sin and all law-breakers, and *throw them into the fiery furnace. In that place there will be weeping and gnashing of teeth.* Then the righteous will shine like the sun in the kingdom of their Father." (vv. 40–43)[3]

These are terrifying statements that Jesus makes. It's difficult to stomach, but the image of "weeping" as the wicked are cast into hell ("the fiery furnace") is common among first-century Jewish writers. Jesus, again, fits right into His own context by using the image here.[4]

Just a few verses later, Jesus says again:

"So it will be at the close of the age. The angels will come out and separate the evil from the righteous and *throw them into the fiery furnace. In that place there will be weeping and gnashing of teeth.*" (vv. 49–50)

The hell that Jesus describes here is not a hell-on-earth that accompanies our bad decisions during this life, and it certainly isn't the never-ending party that AC/DC describes in their song. Hell is a place of punishment at the end of the age for "all law-breakers" who don't follow Jesus in this life.

Again, Jesus said:

> "It is better for you to enter life crippled or lame
> than with two hands or two feet to be thrown into
> the [everlasting] fire. And if your eye causes you
> to sin, tear it out and throw it away. It is better
> for you to enter life with one eye than with two
> eyes to be thrown into the hell [gehenna] of fire."
> (Matt. 18:8–9)

These images of "everlasting fire" and a "hell of fire" were typical in the first century. Jesus used this common vocabulary to convey an unmistakable message—no Jew would have scratched his head wondering what Jesus was getting at. The everlasting fire of gehenna is a place of punishment for all who don't follow Jesus in this life.

Like other Jewish writers of His day, Jesus also used the image of "darkness" to describe hell. In Matthew 8, He says:

> "I tell you, many will come from east and west and
> recline at table with Abraham, Isaac, and Jacob
> in the kingdom of heaven, while the sons of the
> kingdom will be thrown into the *outer darkness*. In

that place there will be weeping and gnashing of
teeth." (vv. 11–12)

This passage is a critique against Jewish people who think that
their ethnicity can solidify a place in the kingdom. Strikingly, Jesus
says that many Gentiles (those from "east and west") will come into
the kingdom, while many Jews (the "sons of the kingdom") will
not enter because they didn't follow Jesus.[5] Jesus uses stock Jewish
images of "outer darkness" and "weeping" to refer to judgment day
and its consequences. Nobody in Jesus' first-century world would
understand these images of darkness and weeping in any other way,
as we saw in the last chapter.

Jesus used the same imagery at the end of another parable He
told just before He died:

"Then the king said to the attendants, 'Bind
him hand and foot and cast him into the outer
darkness. In that place there will be weeping and
gnashing of teeth.'" (Matt. 22:13)

And again, in another parable:

"And cast out the worthless servant into the
outer darkness. In that place there will be

weeping and gnashing of teeth."
(Matt. 25:30)


Darkness, weeping, and gnashing of teeth—these are common Jewish images for hell. And again Jesus is referring to a place of punishment, much like His first-century contemporaries. It's also important to recognize that there is nothing in these passages that holds out hope for a second, third, or fourth chance for repentance after death.

The next category is more difficult to assess. Did Jesus believe that the wicked would be annihilated or suffer never-ending punishment in hell?


### Hell Is a Place of Annihilation or Never-Ending Punishment

At times, Jesus seems to imply that hell won't last very long. "Fear him who can *destroy* both soul and body in hell," Jesus says (Matt. 10:28). *Destroy,* not burn forever. This language of destruction is common not only in Jesus' words but also throughout Paul's letters (see chapter 4). However, there is one significant passage in which Jesus seems to speak of hell as a place of never-ending punishment, where unbelievers will suffer horrific, agonizing pain.

Before we move on, though, let me give two words of warning.

First, I believe it is beneficial to dive into the precise meaning of Greek words and grammar, but it may be more technical than some are used to. While the English text is clear, I think it would be good to show that the Greek text supports our English translation.

The issue at stake is crucial and demands nothing less than rigorous, humble, and intense study of God's infallible Word. So we'll need to slow down, roll up our sleeves, and dig into some key texts for the rest of this chapter.

Second, let's not lose sight of what we're talking about. If all we do is believe we've figured out the duration of hell and leave unchanged, then we've failed. With that in mind, let's get back to the Bible, but with the solemn sense that this is real stuff we're reading about. These words have real implications for real people with real destinies.

On several occasions, Jesus said things that may suggest a never-ending punishment, though these passages in themselves are inconclusive. For instance, as we have seen, Jesus says the wicked will be thrown into "everlasting fire" (Matt. 18:8), but is it the fire or the suffering that is everlasting? The passage doesn't specify. Also, in Mark 9, Jesus describes the fire of hell as being "unquenchable ... where their worm does not die" (vv. 44, 48). This may refer to never-ending punishment, but here, too, we have to be careful. Jesus is alluding to Isaiah 66:24 with this imagery (undying worm, unquenchable fire), and Isaiah was probably not thinking of everlasting punishment.[6] Another passage that is sometimes cited to prove never-ending punishment is the parable of the rich man and Lazarus in Luke 16. But this passage doesn't refer to the final state of the wicked—only to a temporary state where the wicked await judgment.[7]

In almost every passage where Jesus mentions hell, He doesn't explicitly say that it will last forever. He speaks of torment, and we get the impression that hell is terrible, that it's a place to be avoided at all costs, but He doesn't clearly tell us how long it will last.

Jesus' most suggestive statement—perhaps His only statement—
about the duration of hell comes in Matthew 25. In this passage,
Jesus speaks of the final judgment that will take place at His second
coming (v. 31). The sheep (believers in Jesus) and goats (unbelievers)
are divided in two camps, and Jesus decides who's who based on what
they've done in their lives. The sheep have served Jesus by clothing
the naked, feeding the hungry, giving drink to the thirsty, and so on,
while the goats did none of these things. Jesus then gives His verdict:

> "Then he will say to those on his left, 'Depart from
> me, you cursed, into the *everlasting fire* prepared
> for the devil and his angels.'" (v. 41)

Jesus reviews their behavior on earth and finds convicting evidence for their condemnation (vv. 42–44) and then concludes:

> "'Truly, I say to you, as you did not do it to
> one of the least of these, you did not do it to
> me.' And these will go away into *everlasting
> punishment*, but the righteous into everlasting
> life." (vv. 45–46)

The two key phrases are *everlasting fire* (v. 41) and *everlasting
punishment* (v. 46). A simple reading of these phrases seems to

infer that hell is never ending. But before we race to this conclusion, we've got to look closely at the Greek words lying behind the English translation, because it's been argued that they don't actually mean what the translations say. For instance, some people who say that hell won't last forever argue that the Greek words translated "everlasting punishment"—*aionios kolasis*—do not mean that the punishment is never ending. Instead, some have argued that *aionios* means "a period of time" while *kolasis* is a term from horticulture that means "pruning" or "trimming." For example:

An *aionios* of *kolasis.* Depending on how you translate *aionios* and *kolasis,* then, the phrase can mean "a period of pruning" or "a time of trimming," or an intense experience of correction.[8]

The argument goes like this: The purpose of "correction" or "pruning," of course, is to improve something, to bring out its fullest potential. Or in this context, to correct the wicked of their bad behavior until they are no longer wicked. So according to this argument, Jesus is not talking about an everlasting punishment for the wicked here, but rather a time of correction so that those enduring punishment will ultimately be saved.[9] During this time, there may be "endless opportunities in an endless amount of time for people to say yes to God."[10]

Part of me wants to believe that this is true. This argument appears to reconcile God's love with Jesus' harsh words about hell.

But is this what the words *aionios kolasis* actually mean? Is this what Jesus is speaking of in Matthew 25:46?

I don't think so, and here's why. Let's first deal with the word *kolasis*. Does it refer to *correction* or *punishment?* For three reasons, the word means "punishment."

First, the word *kolasis* is only used three other times in the New Testament, and in all three passages it clearly means punishment. It is also used in Jewish literature around the time of the New Testament in the same way.[11] Jesus' Jewish audience would have heard Jesus say "punishment" not "correction" when He said the word *kolasis*.[12]

Second, this "everlasting punishment" (*aionios kolasis*) is the same place as the "everlasting fire prepared for the devil and his angels" from verse 41. This is where the goats, or unbelievers, are cast. If one thinks that unbelievers will undergo a time of correction-to-be-saved in that place, one must also say the same thing of the Devil and his angels. But this would be a huge stretch, especially in light of Revelation 19—20, where it says that the Devil and his angels will be tormented forever and ever. So Jesus actually says that unbelievers share the same fate as the Devil and his demons.

Third, as we have seen, Jesus often refers to "hell" or "the fiery furnace" or "everlasting fire" as a place of *retribution*—a place where sinners will be punished for their sins. And Jesus is not talking about correction in these other passages (Matt. 13:41–42, 49–50). So those who say that hell is corrective must argue that Jesus has something very different in mind when He talks about "everlasting fire" and "everlasting *kolasis*" here in Matthew 25:46. But this is very unlikely.

I checked ten commentators from different theological backgrounds and fifteen Bible translations in five different languages on the word *kolasis*. I really wanted to see if other Bible scholars agree with what I said above. I found that they all translate *kolasis* with the word "punishment" (or *strafe*, or *castigo*, or наказание, or 刑).[13] Translators and commentators are not infallible, but such a diverse and worldwide consensus should raise serious caution.

It seems clear that Jesus was referring to an "*aionios* punishment" in Matthew 25:46, and not an "*aionios* correction."

What about the word *aionios?* Bible scholars have debated the meaning of this term for what seems like an eternity, so we're not going to settle the issue here.[14] It's important to note that however we translate *aionios,* the passage still refers to punishment for the wicked, which is something that Universalists deny.

Simply put, *aionios* can mean various things, including "lifelong," "enduring," or "everlasting." When the word is used twice in Matthew 25:46 ("*aionios* life" and "*aionios* punishment"), it probably means "everlasting" in both cases.[15] I say this for two reasons.

First, the contrast between "*aionios* life" and "*aionios* punishment" includes the notion of never-ending time. While it is true that *aionios* doesn't always mean "everlasting," when used here to describe things in the "age to come," it probably does have this meaning. Think about it: *Because* the life in this age will never end, given the parallel, it also seems that the punishment in this age will never end.

Second, the punishment is said to be in the "everlasting [*aionios*] fire prepared for the devil and his angels" (Matt. 25:41). We know from other passages in Scripture that the Devil and his angels will suffer *never-ending punishment* (Rev. 20:10). Therefore, when Jesus says that unbelievers will go to the same place and suffer the same punishment, it logically follows that their punishment will also never end.[16]

## So Where Do I Land?

The debate about hell's duration is much more complex than I first assumed. While I lean heavily on the side that says it is everlasting, I am not ready to claim that with complete certainty. I encourage you to continue researching, but don't get so caught up in this debate that you miss the point of what Jesus was trying to communicate. I even deleted several pages that I wrote about the issue because I feared it would distract from the heart of Christ's message.

Jesus chose strong and terrifying language when He spoke of hell. I believe He chose to speak this way because He loves us and wanted to warn us. So let's not miss the point: He spoke of hell as a horrifying place, characterized by suffering, fire, darkness, and lamentation. I believe His intention was to stir a fear in us that would cause us to take hell seriously and avoid it at all costs.

I was a bit surprised at how many harsh statements Jesus made about hell. It probably caught me off guard because I am so used to people emphasizing His words of blessing, not His words of warning. Some of His words may have shocked you, but I would like you to consider the following thought:

We are bound by the words of the Creator, the One who will do what is right. The One who invented justice and knows perfectly what the unbeliever deserves. God has never asked us to figure out His justice or to see if His way of doing things is morally right. He has only asked us to embrace His Word and bow the knee, to tremble at His word, as Isaiah says (66:2).

Don't get so lost in deciphering that you forget to tremble.

## Notes

1.  Despite the ESV's translation, I will be using the term *everlast-ing* instead of *eternal,* because the latter term technically means transcending time, which isn't the best rendering of the Greek *aionios.* See the discussion toward the end of this chapter and in note 14 below.

2.  Bell, *Love Wins,* 73.

3.  This will happen at a future time when Christ comes back and everyone will stand before Him in judgment. The righteous will be resurrected (which is the meaning of "shine like the sun," cf. Dan. 12:2), and the wicked will be thrown into the "fiery furnace," an image that depicts hell (The two references to the "fiery furnace" in Matthew 13 are the only times that this image is used of hell in the New Testament. However, Revelation 9:2 uses a similar image, where smoke goes up from a great furnace [R. T. France, *The Gospel of Matthew,* 537].). The phrase *gnashing of teeth* is used quite often by Jesus (see Matt. 8:12; 22:13; 24:51; 25:30; Luke 13:28), though we don't need to take it literally—as if a toothless unbeliever will have teeth provided on judgment day. The phrase probably depicts the pain that the wicked will experi-ence in hell.

4.  See e.g., *1 En.* 108:3–5; *2 En.* 40:12.

5.  In the New Testament, the kingdom has both a present and future aspect. Many times the idea of entering the kingdom refers to something that happens in the present. Other times the idea refers to something that will happen after death or after the second coming of Christ. In this passage (Matt. 8), it's the future aspect of entering the kingdom that is in view.

6.  In Isaiah's context, the worm doesn't die as it eats the flesh of dead bodies. There's nothing in the context that says the souls of the dead are still being tormented. The image of worms feasting on unburied dead people emphasizes the shame of defeat.

7.  The parable of the rich man and Lazarus (Luke 16:19–31) says that the rich man goes to "Hades" while Lazarus goes to "Abraham's bosom" (NASB). Hades here should not be confused with hell. Hades is where the wicked go to await their judgment, after which they are thrown into hell—their final state. Lazarus is also in some sort of intermediate state where he is waiting for his resurrection. Significantly, the rich man, who's in hades, is "in agony in this flame" (16:24 NASB), and he's very aware of it. Moreover, Jesus says that there is a chasm that separates the wicked from the righteous and "none may cross from there to us" (16:26). So this passage affirms that there will be some sort of punishment and torment for the wicked immediately upon death, and there is no sign that these situations can be reversed. This intermediate state for the wicked should not be confused with the Roman Catholic doctrine of

purgatory, which has a very different function from what we see in Luke 16. So Luke 16 doesn't refer to the duration of hell.

Now, it's true that this is a parable, and so we shouldn't press the details too far. Jesus uses the parable in this context of Luke to confront the social structures of the day, not to teach us about the afterlife. On the flip side, parables do convey truth—real things about real life for real people. And given the fact that at least some first-century Jewish people believed that there would be real pain and torment in hades (and not just in gehenna or "hell"), Jesus was probably assuming this view here as well. According to Josephus, the Pharisees believed that the righteous receive rewards and the wicked receive punishment immediately after they die (*Ant.* 18.14). Also, *4 Ezra* 7:78–87 (ca. AD 100) says that there will be punishment in the intermediate sate (i.e., hades).

8. Bell, *Love Wins,* 91. Bell's original quote transliterated the Greek words as *aion* (a noun) and *kalazo* (a verb). But the Greek actually has *aionios* (an adjective) and *kolasis* (a noun). For clarity, I changed the words in Bell's quote to reflect the Greek of Matthew. New Testament scholar William Barclay also says that *kolasis* "originally meant the pruning of trees to make them grow better. I think it is true to say that in all Greek secular literature *kolasis* is never used of anything but remedial punishment" (*A Spiritual Autobiography* [Grand Rapids, MI: Eerdmans, 1977], 66). But see note 11 below.

9. Bell, *Love Wins,* 92–93.

10. Ibid., 106–107.

11. The noun is used in 1 John 4:18. Here, John says that "there is no fear in love, but perfect love casts out fear. For fear has to do with punishment (*kolasis*)." The context here is "the day of judgment" (v. 17), and John is contrasting love with fear. Love enables one to be confident on the day of judgment (v. 17), while fear instills that nagging sense that one will receive *punishment* (*kolasis*) on the day of judgment. The sense of "correction" wouldn't make sense. The verb form of *kolasis* (*kolazo*) is used two times in the New Testament: Acts 4:21 and 2 Peter 2:9. Both of these contexts demand that the word be translated "punishment." For its use in Jewish literature, see especially Wis. 16:1–2, where the verb *kolazo* is used synonymously with the verb *basanizo*, which means torment. Retributive punishment is clearly in view. See also *T. Reub.* 5:5; *T. Gad* 7:5 (though these texts have been edited by Christians). A related Hebrew expression is used throughout the Dead Sea Scrolls to mean punishment as well (see 1QS 2:15; 5:13; 1QM 1:5; 9:5–6; 4Q510 1:7). See W. D. Davies and Dale C. Allison Jr., *Matthew* (The International Critical Commentary) (Edinburgh: T & T Clark, 2004), 3.432.

12. Of course, Jesus would have used the Aramaic equivalent to this word, but this is the Greek word that Matthew (under the inspiration of the Holy Spirit) used to translate Jesus' word.

13. Commentaries: Leon Morris, *The Gospel According to Matthew* (Piller New Testament Commentary) (Grand Rapids, MI:

Eerdmans, 1992), 641; Davies and Allison, *Matthew,* 3.432; R. T. France, *The Gospel of Matthew,* 966–967; D. A. Hagner, *Matthew 14—28* (Word Biblical Commentary 33b) (Nashville, TN: Thomas Nelson, 1995), 2.746; Craig Keener, *A Commentary on the Gospel of Matthew* (Grand Rapids, MI: Eerdmans, 1999), 606; Ulrich Luz, *Matthew: A Commentary,* trans. W. C. Linss (Minneapolis, MN.: Augsburg Fortress Press, 2005), 282; Grant Osborne, *Matthew: Exegetical Commentary on the New Testament* (Grand Rapids, MI: Zondervan, 2010), 938–939; D. A. Carson, *Matthew* (The Expositor's Bible Commentary) (Grand Rapids, MI: Zondervan, 2010), 586–587; Robert Mounce, *Matthew* (New International Biblical Commentary) (Peabody, MA: Hendrickson, 1991), 236–237; Michael Wilkins, *Matthew* (The NIV Application Commentary) (Grand Rapids, MI: Zondervan, 2004), 812–813. Translations: ESV, TNIV, NASB, HCSB, NKJV, NLT, CEB, AMP, CEV, GNT. Foreign translations: *Hoffnung für Alle; Nueva Traducción Viviente; Slovo Zhizny; Chinese Union Version (Traditional and Simplified). The Message* has "eternal doom," which is essentially the same thing.

14. The Greek word *aionios* is an adjective, and it's used seventy times in the New Testament. The noun, *aion,* is used over one hundred times in the New Testament. The noun can mean various things such as "an age" or "era" (Matt. 13:39; 28:20; Heb. 9:26; 1 Cor. 10:11), "the world" (Mark 4:19), and the never-ending "age" to come, as it does so often in John's gospel (John 4:14; 6:51, 58; 8:35, 51; 10:28; 11:26; 12:34; 14:16). The adjective *aionios* frequently means "everlasting," denoting

never-ending time. We see this sense in the phrase "everlasting life" (*aionios zoe*) used so often in the New Testament
(Matt. 19:16; Luke 10:25; 16:9; Rom. 2:7; 5:21; 6:22; 16:25;
Gal. 6:8; 1 Tim. 1:16; 6:12, 16; 2 Tim. 2:10; Jude 21). This
understanding of time does not refer to the Platonic notion of
timelessness, which is inherent in the term *eternity*, but to the
duration of the age to come—a vibrant Jewish concept of the
future. Because this age to come will last forever, the adjective *aionios,* when describing this age, often connotes this idea
of "everlasting" as well. For a full and quite technical discussion, see Joachim Guhrt, "Time," in Colin Brown, ed., *New
International Dictionary of New Testament Theology* (Grand
Rapids, MI: Zondervan, 1986): 3.826–33; Hermann Sasse,
"*aion, aionios,*" in Gerhard Kittel, ed., *Theological Dictionary
of the New Testament* (Grand Rapids, MI: Eerdmans, 1985),
1.197–209. I thank Drs. Simon Gathercole of Cambridge
University and Scott Hafemann of St. Andrews for their very
helpful and critical comments on previous drafts of this discussion of *aionios*.

15. Contra Bell, *Love Wins,* 91–92.

16. The way the Greek words are used here suggests a never-ending
    punishment. The word *aionios* modifies the nature of the pun-
    ishment, not the results of the punishment. This is an important
    distinction, because some people say that it's only the results of
    the punishment that never end. In other words, some say that
    the wicked will be annihilated as they are punished, and this

annihilation is never-ending in the sense that its results cannot be reversed. But *aionios* modifies *kalasis,* which is a noun
of action (the root is *kolasis*). Greek nouns that end with *–sis*
(rather than *–ma*) tend to focus on the action of the noun rather
than its results. For the small handful of people still reading this
note, you can look at 2 Thess. 2:16 in the Greek to see a parallel, where *aionios* modifies *paraklesis* ("comfort"), another *–sis*
ending noun of action. Here again, it is the never-ending act of
comforting that is in view.

# Chapter 4

# What Jesus' Followers Said about Hell

As we saw in the last chapter, Jesus agreed with His Jewish contemporaries about the realities of hell. But what about the people who came after Jesus? Did they imitate His example in speaking openly about the punishment of the wicked? This is a very important question to answer for a couple of reasons. First, it makes it much easier to come to conclusions if other New Testament writers made statements similar to those of Jesus. Second, it helps us understand the example that was set for us. In other words, if Jesus and His early followers spoke boldly about hell, then shouldn't we do the same?

So in this chapter, we will explore some other books and letters in the New Testament and see what they say about hell.

## Hell in the Letters of Paul, Peter, and Jude

We'll start by examining Paul's view of hell. But the first thing to notice is that he never used the word. Did you get that? Paul *never* in all of his thirteen letters used the word *hell.* If you only focused on that one truth, you might conclude that Paul avoided the issue.

And yet, Paul referred to the fate of the wicked more than any other New Testament writer did. Though he never used the actual word *hell,* he did speak of "death" as the result of sin, whereby the wicked would "perish" or "be destroyed" by the "wrath" of God. The sinner, according to Paul, stands "condemned" and will be "judged" by God on account of his sin. And unless the sinner repents and turns to Christ, he will be "punished" by God when Christ returns. Paul described the fate of the wicked with words such as "perish, destroy, wrath, punish," and others more than eighty times in his thirteen letters.[1] To put this in perspective, Paul made reference to the fate of the wicked more times in his letters than he mentioned God's forgiveness, mercy, or heaven combined.[2] So even though Paul never used the actual word *hell,* nor did he describe the place with any detail, he assuredly believed that the wicked will face a horrific fate if they remain in their sin.

One would have to be creative and work hard to erase all notions of wrath and punishment from the letters of Paul.

I have always been convicted by Paul's efforts to reach unbelievers. At times, I have even felt guilty when reading of the suffering he endured in sharing the gospel. When I read what he writes about the punishment of the wicked, it helps me understand how he stayed so motivated. Could it be that his drive to reach the lost was directly related to his willingness to ponder their fate if he didn't reach them at all? It sure appears so.

This would explain Paul's strange sermon in Acts 17. In this chapter, we find Paul standing before a strictly pagan (rather than Jewish) audience, who wouldn't have had any knowledge of Jesus, the Old Testament, the God of Israel, or any other connecting points to the gospel. Paul stands up, and he's got only minutes to deliver a message, to share the good news with them. What does he do? He speaks of judgment. He mentions plenty of other things, and he even quotes a few of their own poets (v. 28), but when it came to the punch line, Paul told them that God would judge them if they didn't repent:

> "God ... commands all people everywhere to
> repent, because he has fixed a day on which he will
> judge the world in righteousness by a man whom
> he has appointed; and of this he has given assurance
> to all by raising him from the dead." (vv. 30–31)

There's no cross, no atonement, no forgiveness, no conversion testimony, and no God-loves-you-and-has-a-wonderful-plan-for-your-life. Not that these things are unnecessary—Paul himself will talk about these on other occasions. But what these people needed to hear most was that Jesus has been raised from the dead and was going to judge them if they didn't repent.

Like most of you, I get annoyed at those street preachers who carry on about wrath and judgment—I wish they'd talk more about grace and love. Sometimes I wonder if they do more harm than good. Yet as I sit back and arrogantly judge their effectiveness, I must admit that Paul's sermon in Acts 17 sounds an awful lot like the preacher I heard screaming at the beach last week!

The point is this: While much of our church culture believes that talk of wrath and judgment is toxic and unloving, Paul didn't seem to have a problem with these things. In fact, Paul believed that these were essential truths. Similar to John the Baptist and Jesus, Paul believed that warning people of the wrath to come was actually loving. If my two-year-old son runs out into the street, is it unloving to warn him of the destruction coming in the form of a Chevy 4x4? Does anyone criticize the fireman for waking up a family to rescue them from a burning house? Does anyone blame a doctor for telling a person that he has cancer that must be treated if he is going to live?

No doubt, many Christians have abused the ideas of judgment and wrath. One of the first sermons I ever understood, I heard when I was twelve years old. A preacher screamed from stage about the horrors of hell. He then warned us not to reject Jesus—and his exact words were, "It would be better for you to bite your tongue off and spit it out!" We have probably all been exposed to one of those preachers, who can't wait to tell everyone to repent, who only talks about judgment and wrath, yet never mentions love, forgiveness, compassion, and mercy. The Bible paints a much bigger picture of God, life, and the gospel than mere judgment and the need for repentance. Remember, it's "good" news.

But just because some have swung the pendulum so far in the direction of wrath and judgment, let's not swing it back too far the other direction and do away with what Scripture emphasizes. God is compassionate and just, loving and holy, wrathful and forgiving. We can't sideline His more difficult attributes to make room for the palatable ones.

Now back to Paul.

I said earlier that Paul never wrote about the details of hell. However, there is one passage where he comes pretty close—a passage blistering with passion and urgency about Christ's second coming and the wrath that follows:

> God considers it just to repay with affliction those
> who afflict you, and to grant relief to you who
> are afflicted as well as to us, when the Lord Jesus
> is revealed from heaven with his mighty angels in
> flaming fire, inflicting vengeance on those who
> do not know God and on those who do not obey
> the gospel of our Lord Jesus. They will suffer the
> punishment of eternal destruction, away from the
> presence of the Lord and from the glory of his
> might. (2 Thess. 1:6–9)

There are several things to note in this passage. First, the wrath of Jesus here is *retributive* and not *corrective*. In other words, the wrath isn't intended to correct the behavior of those opposing

Christ to make them fit for salvation. Rather, the wrath is an act of—dare I say—vengeance. In fact, this is the exact word that Paul uses. Christ will "inflict vengeance on those who do not know God" and don't "obey the gospel of our Lord Jesus."[3] Second, in light of this last phrase, Paul doesn't have a select group of people in view. Those who don't know God or obey the gospel include everyone not following Jesus. No matter how innocent some people may seem, Paul says that if they don't know God or obey the gospel, they will face God's vengeful wrath when Jesus returns.[4]

As I read those verses, I am struck by how allergic I am to repeating the very words that Paul wrote. Affliction, vengeance, punishment, destruction—for all who don't follow Jesus. I'm not sure if I have ever used the term *vengeance* in describing the fate of unbelievers. In my desire to distance myself from sadistic Christians who revel in the idea of wrath and punishment, I may have crossed a line. Refusing to teach a passage of Scripture is just as wrong as abusing it.

I really believe it's time for some of us to stop apologizing *for* God and start apologizing *to* Him for being embarrassed by the ways He has chosen to reveal Himself.

## Hell in 2 Peter and Jude

Apart from those of Paul, two other letters speak extensively of wrath and judgment. In fact, 2 Peter 2 alone looks like a chapter out of Dante's *Inferno,* while the book of Jude reads like a medieval tract written to scare peasants into unwavering church attendance and a steady tithe. These books together speak of "destruction" (2

Peter 2:1, 3, 12; 3:7, 9; Jude 5, 10, 11), "punishment" (2 Peter 2:9; Jude 7), "judgment" (2 Peter 2:4, 9; Jude 4), "condemnation" (2 Peter 2:3; Jude 4), "hell"[5] (2 Peter 2:4), and retributive suffering (2 Peter 2:13) that await the ungodly who don't follow Jesus. Hell is described as "the gloom of utter darkness" (2 Peter 2:17; Jude 13) and the "punishment of eternal fire" (Jude 7, 23), terms that would be very familiar, as we have seen, in the authors' Jewish contexts.[6]

Now, these books emphasize that hell is reserved for evil angels and false teachers, who indulge in fleshly desires and distort the gospel for financial gain (2 Peter 2:1, 4, 15–16). But both authors affirm that the same punishment is in store for all unrighteous people (2 Peter 2:9; Jude 14–15). As much as these terrifying images of wrath and hell are unpleasant to read, they do capture an important part of the Christian message: God will severely punish those who don't bow the knee to King Jesus.

## Hell in Revelation

But even 2 Peter and Jude don't match John's description of hell in the book of Revelation. So to the final book we turn.

The first passage where we see a depiction of hell is Revelation 14. Speaking of the final judgment of God, the author writes:

> "If anyone worships the beast and its image and
> receives a mark on his forehead or on his hand, he

also will drink the wine of God's wrath, poured
full strength into the cup of his anger, and he will
be tormented with fire and sulfur in the presence
of the holy angels and in the presence ... of the
Lamb. And the smoke of their torment goes up
forever and ever, and they have no rest, day or
night, these worshipers of the beast and its image,
and whoever receives the mark of its name." (vv.
9–11)

The idea of "God's wrath" and "anger," along with the image of
being "tormented with fire and sulfur ... forever and ever," is terrifying.[7] But that seems to be an important theme in Revelation: *God's
wrath is terrifying!* John isn't trying to resolve the tension between
this potent imagery of punishment and the loving God who dies
for His enemies as described in Romans 5. Instead, John gives us a
powerful warning: Don't oppose God!

Most terrifying is the nature of the punishment—it's ongoing
with no end in sight. Not only does John say that people will be
"tormented with fire" (rather than destroyed),[8] but he goes on to
say that the smoke of their torment goes up "forever and ever." And
just to drive home the point, he adds the phrase "they have no rest,
day or night."[9]

Again, it's very easy to get caught up in arguments and word
studies and theological views, and yet miss the main point. This is
real. We're talking about the fate of actual people. Let's keep that in
mind as we look at one more passage in Revelation.

In the final chapters of the book, we are given a picture of what will happen after Christ comes back. John depicts a blessed, never-ending age of peace, joy, and victory for all who "follow the Lamb." No death, no sadness, no fear, no evil, no pain, no tears—only an ongoing blissful life with the Creator in His new creation (21:1; 22:1–2). This is the destiny of all who follow Him.

But there is also a future for all who don't follow Him. Here's how the author describes it:

> The devil who had deceived them was thrown into
> the lake of fire and sulfur where the beast and the
> false prophet were, and they will be tormented day
> and night forever and ever. (Rev. 20:10)

As you read that verse, keep in mind that the Devil is one of God's created beings. Sometimes we hide behind questions like "how could a good God create someone and then torment that person forever?" Yet few people deny that He does this to Satan. Some even rejoice in this. John then describes a judgment scene where he sees

> the dead, great and small, standing before the
> throne, and books were opened … and the dead
> were judged by what was written in the books,
> according to what they had done … and they were

judged, each one of them, according to what they
had done. Then Death and Hades were thrown
into the lake of fire. This is the second death, the
lake of fire. And if anyone's name was not found
written in the book of life, he was thrown into the
lake of fire. (20:12–15)

Even though it's the Devil, beast, and false prophet who will be
"tormented day and night forever and ever" in the lake of fire, John
says that unbelievers go to the same place. If they go to the same
place, they probably suffer the same fate—never-ending punishment in the lake of fire. John says again in the next chapter,

But as for the cowardly, the faithless, the
detestable, as for murderers, the sexually immoral,
sorcerers, idolaters, and all liars, their portion
will be in the lake that burns with fire and sulfur,
which is the second death. (21:8)

The lake of fire is the final destiny for *both* the Devil and unbelievers. We have already seen that the phrase "tormented day and
night forever and ever" refers to a never-ending punishment for the
wicked. The same phrase "forever and ever" is used to describe the
"reign" of God's people, which will never end (Rev. 22:5). This is
further supported by Revelation 22:14 where those redeemed by

Christ (i.e., "those who wash their robes") live in the new creation, while "outside are the dogs and sorcerers and the sexually immoral and murderers and idolaters, and everyone who loves and practices falsehood" (v. 15). This passage depicts an ongoing separation between believers who live in the presence of God (v. 14) and unbelievers who live "outside," or apart from the presence of God in the new creation.

So why is the lake of fire called the second "death" if its punishment is ongoing? Doesn't this point to a final annihilation and not an ongoing torment for the wicked? While the word *death* itself could suggest finality, it is often used throughout the New Testament in a more metaphorical (nonliteral) sense. For instance, New Testament writers often refer to unbelievers as "dead" (referring to their spiritual state), even though they are physically alive (Luke 15:24, 32; Eph. 2:1, 12; Col. 2:13). Also, we already saw that the phrases *forever and ever, torment,* and *day and night* (Rev. 14:10–11; 20:10) point to something that has no end in sight. So it seems best to understand the word *death* not in terms of total annihilation but as a description of those who will be separated from God forever in an ongoing state of punishment.

An ongoing … state … of punishment …

For all who don't love Jesus.

What causes my heart to ache right now as I'm writing this is that my life shows little evidence that I actually believe this. Every time my thoughts wander to the future of unbelievers, I quickly brush them aside so they don't ruin my day. But there is a reality here that I can't ignore. Even as the conversations of people around me fill my ears, the truth of Scripture penetrates my heart with sobering statements about their destinies. We can talk about the fate of some hypothetical person, but as I look up and see their smiles, I have to ask myself if I really believe what I have written in this book. Hell is for real. *Am I?*

I would love to think, as some have suggested, that the Bible doesn't actually say a whole lot about hell. I would love to stare at my friend's face when he asked that question we all fear— "Do you think I'm going to hell?"—and say "No! There is no such place! Jesus loves you and wants to heal your pain and turn your sorrows into gladness!"

But the New Testament writers didn't have the same allergic reaction to hell as I do. Perhaps they had a view of God that is much bigger than mine. A view of God that takes Him at His word and doesn't try to make Him fit our own moral standards and human sentimentality. A view of God that believes what He says, even when it doesn't make perfect sense to us.

# Notes

1. Here's the references for the individual words: "death" or "die" (Greek: *apothnesko, thanatos;* Rom. 1:32; 5:12, 14, 15, 17, 21; 6:16, 21, 23; 7:5, 9, 10, 11, 13; 8:2, 6, 13; 1 Cor. 15:21, 22; 2 Cor. 2:16; 3:6, 7; 7:10; Eph. 2:1); "perish," "destroy," "destruction" (Greek: *apollymi, apoleia, olethros, phthora;* Rom. 2:12; 9:22; 14:15, 20; 1 Cor. 1:18; 15:18; 2 Cor. 2:15; 4:3; Gal. 6:8; Phil. 1:28; 3:19; 1 Thess. 5:3; 2 Thess. 1:9; 2:10; 1 Tim. 6:9); "wrath" (Greek: *orge, thymos;* Rom. 1:18; 2:5, 8; 3:5; 5:9; 9:22; Eph. 2:3; 5:6; Col. 3:6; 1 Thess. 1:10; 2:16; 5:9); "condemn," "condemnation," or "judge" (Greek: several words with the root *krin-;* Rom. 2:1, 2, 3, 5, 12; 3:7, 8; 5:16, 18; 8:1; 1 Cor. 11:32; 2 Cor. 3:9; 2 Thess. 2:12; 1 Tim. 5:24); "curse," "cursed" (Greek: *anathema, katara;* Rom. 9:3; Gal. 1:8, 9; 3:10, 13; 1 Cor. 12:3; 16:22); "punish" (Greek: *ekdikos, ekdikesis, dike;* 1 Thess. 4:6; 2 Thess. 1:8, 9). For all these references, see Douglas Moo, "Paul on Hell," in Christopher W. Morgan and Robert A. Peterson, eds., *Hell Under Fire: Modern Scholarship Reinvents Eternal Punishment* (Grand Rapids, MI: Zondervan, 2004), 92–93.

2. Paul uses Greek words (verbs and nouns) for "mercy" twenty-seven times, "forgiveness" seven times, and the noun "heaven" twenty-one times. This word search was performed through the recent (and quite excellent) Bible program Scroll Tag (ScrollTag.com).

3.  Paul here is alluding to Isaiah 66:14–16, where God will "show his indignation against his enemies" (v. 14), "render his anger in fury, and his rebuke with flames of fire" (v. 15), and "by fire will the LORD enter into judgment … with all flesh" (v. 16). The aftermath is sobering: "those slain by the LORD shall be many" (v. 16). Throughout this passage, Isaiah describes God's future punishment of those who reject Him. God will "choose harsh treatment for" those who "did not listen" to God's offer of salvation (v. 4).

4.  In this passage, Paul uses the phrase *everlasting destruction*. Does this mean Paul affirms that unbelievers will live forever in never-ending torment? Or does he mean that unbelievers will be annihilated when Christ comes back? This verse is not crystal clear, and anyone who thinks it is needs a good dose of interpretative humility. On the one hand, the word *destruction* seems to speak of annihilation. But Paul says it's "everlasting," so some have said that Paul is thinking of never-ending punishment in hell. However, as we have seen, the word *everlasting* (*aionios*) doesn't always mean "never-ending." Even if it does mean never-ending here, it would seem to make better sense that the "never ending-ness" speaks of the results or effects of the destruction rather than its ongoing act. In other words, I don't think Paul is referring to the never-ending process of God "destroying but not completely destroying" the wicked in hell here. At least Paul's words here don't clearly convey this notion. Neither, however, does Paul clearly say that the wicked *will be* annihilated and *will not* suffer ongoing

punishment. There is evidence that first-century writers use phrases like *eternal destruction* and actually do mean the act of punishment that never ends. Therefore, while Paul makes a clear point about punishment, vengeance, retribution, and wrath, he doesn't speak unambiguously about the duration of this wrath.

5.   The word Peter uses for "hell" here is the Greek *tartarus*. This term is used in Greek mythology to refer to the place where giants such as Cyclops and the Titans were cast. *Tartarus* is also used in Hellenistic, or Greek, branches of Judaism, as seen, for instance, in the Septuagint of Job (40:20; 41:24), Proverbs (30:16), and other early Jewish writers (e.g., *Sib. Or.* 4:186; *1 En.* 20:2; Philo, *Mos.* 2.433; *Praem.* 152). For a discussion, see Richard Bauckham, *2 Peter and Jude* (Word Bible Commentary 50) (Waco, TX: Word, 1983), 249.

6.   As with Paul, I don't think Peter and Jude are very clear about the duration of hell. On the one hand, both books are laced with the language of destruction, which in itself suggests annihilation. On the other hand, the phrase *punishment of eternal fire* (Jude 7, 23) could refer to ongoing torment, though, as we have seen before, it doesn't have to. Therefore, again, I think we have to be cautious about pressing the language to support either annihilation or never-ending punishment. In any case, neither book holds out hope that those who meet God's wrath in the end with have other opportunities after this to repent and be saved.

7.  The identity of the beast and its followers is widely disputed. Some say that the beast refers to Rome, and its followers are those who wave the Roman flag, so to speak. Others say it's the worldly systems and those who embraced them throughout all time. Still others say that the beast is some infamous leader: Hitler, Saddam, bin Laden, and even the Pope are among the top candidates. (I personally think this approach is wrong-headed.) For our purpose, it's not that important to settle on this issue. The beast and its followers under any view refer to those who are not on the side of Jesus, whether in the first century, all centuries, or the final days before Christ comes back. The author here is speaking quite simply of unbelievers. This is confirmed by later passages that refer to unbelievers facing God's future judgment (see Rev. 20:15; 21:8).

8.  The word for "torment," *basanismos,* is never used in Revelation nor in the entire Bible to refer to the annihilation of personal existence. In Revelation, it always refers to conscious suffering (see Rev. 9:5; 11:10; 12:2; 18:7, 10, 15; 20:10; G. K. Beale, *The Book of Revelation: A Commentary on the Greek Text* [New International Greek Testament Commentary] [Grand Rapids, MI: Eerdmans, 1998], 762; contra Edward Fudge, *Fire That Consumes: A Biblical Case for Conditional Immortality,* 2nd ed., rev. Peter Cousins [Carlisle, UK: Paternoster, 1994], 304–307).

9.  The phrase *forever and ever* is used twelve other times in Revelation, eleven of which clearly refer to something that never ends—such as the existence of God, which is "forever and ever"

(Rev. 10:6; 15:7). For all the uses of the phrase in Revelation, see 1:6, 18; 4:9, 10; 5:13; 7:12; 10:6; 11:15; 15:7; 19:3; 20:10; 22:5. For the use of the phrase in the New Testament, see Galatians 1:5; Ephesians 3:21; Philippians 4:20; 1 Timothy 1:17; 2 Timothy 4:18; Hebrews 13:21; 1 Peter 4:11; see David Aune, *Revelation 6—16* (Word Bible Commentary 52B) (Nashville, TN: Thomas Nelson, 1998), 836. The never-ending nature of the punishment is further supported by the phrase *they have no rest, day or night.* Therefore, while the phrase *forever and ever* in itself *could* refer to the intensity of the punishment and not the duration (see Revelation 19:3 where it may refer to the intensity), its dominant use in Revelation and the context of 14:9–11 supports the notion of a never-ending punishment. Moreover, the parallel passage in 20:10–15 refers to a never-ending punishment and uses similar terms to do so. As we will see, this latter passage says that the Devil and false prophet will be "thrown into the lake of fire and sulfur" where they will be "tormented night and day forever and ever" (Rev. 20:10). And this is the same place where all the wicked will go (Rev. 20:15). Both passages, Revelation 14 and 20, have the phrases *torment, night and day,* and *forever and ever,* which suggest that they are speaking of the same ongoing punishment.

# Chapter 5

# What Does This Have to Do with Me?

If you're a Christian and wondering what all of this has to do with you, keep reading.

The other morning, I woke up to start writing as I've been doing for the past few weeks, and I decided to do something different. I closed my laptop and just read through all of these passages on hell.

I didn't think about writing; I didn't try to figure out all the nitty-gritty details of the text. I just let the New Testament speak in its power and simplicity, and here are some of the shocking things that God hit me with.

## You Fool

Jesus threatens hell to those who curse their brother (Matt. 5:22). He's not warning drinkers or smokers or murderers. Jesus preaches hellfire against those who have the audacity to attack a fellow human being with harsh words. It's ironic—frightening, actually—that some people have written books, preached sermons, or written blog posts about hell and missed this point completely. In fact, some people have slammed their Christian brothers and sisters in the process, simply because they have a different view of hell, missing the purpose of Matthew 5: Whoever calls his brother a fool may find himself guilty of hell.

Have you called your brother a fool lately? On a blog? On Facebook? Have you tweeted anything of the sort?

So often these hell passages become fodder for debate, and people miss the point of the warning. Jesus didn't speak of hell so that we could study, debate, and write books about it. He gave us these passages so that we would live holy lives. Stop slandering one another, and live in peace and brotherly unity. Jesus evidently hates it when we tear into our brothers or sisters with demeaning words, words that fail to honor the people around us as the beautiful image-bearing creatures that they are.

## But Jesus, Didn't We ...

And how about Matthew 7, probably the scariest passage on hell in the entire Bible? The most horrific word in this passage isn't *hell;* it isn't *fire, furnace, everlasting, gloom, darkness, worms,* or *torment.* In fact, none of these words occur in this passage. The most frightening word is *many.* Jesus says, *"Many* will say to Me on that day, 'Lord, Lord, did we not prophesy in Your name, and in Your name cast out demons, and in Your name perform many miracles?'" (Matt. 7:22 NASB). This is judgment day. This is the end. There are no second chances. This is the last peaceful breath that "many" will breathe before they spend the rest of their life in hell. Put yourself there for a second. Fast-forward your life to that day. Will you sound like the many who call out in desperation, "Lord, Lord, did I not _____ and _____ and _____ in Your name?"

How will Jesus respond to your laundry list of Christian activities—your Easter services, tithe, Bible studies, church pot-lucks, and summer-camp conversions? Are you sure you're on the right side? What evidence do you have that you *know* Jesus? Please understand my heart. I believe I am asking these questions for the same reason that Jesus gives the warning. It's the most loving thing I can do! "Many" will go to hell even though they thought they'd waltz into paradise. Jesus will say, "I never *knew* you; depart from me" (Matt. 7:23).

## From Every Tribe and Tongue

Or take racism. The Christian church in many ages and in many places has stood on the wrong side of this issue, and it's damnable—literally. *What's racism got to do with hell?* you may ask. According to

Jesus, it's got everything to do with it. In Matthew 8, Jesus smuggles a warning about hell into the context of racism and ethnocentrism (the belief that your ethnicity is superior). The entire context of Matthew 8—9 depicts Jesus reversing all of the cultural and social assumptions of the Jews of that day. One assumption is that the Jews, as the "people of God," are much more fit for the kingdom than all those other nasty sinners—those Gentiles, those Greeks, those Romans. But in Matthew 8, Jesus is absolutely floored by the faith of a *Roman Gentile military leader*. This leader of high standing had the faith and humility to submit to the authority of Jesus. And Jesus accepted him as he is, as a *Gentile*. From this encounter, Jesus spins out a short message about many people of all nations and colors and ethnicities that will flood into the kingdom. And it is here that Jesus says that the "sons of the kingdom" who think that God values one ethnicity over another (in this case, the Jewish people) are damned to hell: "The sons of the kingdom shall be cast out into the outer darkness; in that place there shall be weeping and gnashing of teeth" (Matt. 8:12 NASB). The teeth that once gnashed at the person of another race or color will gnash in the agony of eternal torment.

Why is it that only 5.5 percent of American evangelical churches could be considered multiethnic (where no single ethnicity makes up more than 80 percent of its congregants)?[1] Why is that? Five and a half percent! And we're supposed to be living in the melting pot, the place where hundreds of languages and colors often live within a few miles—or feet—of each other. What's so sad about this is that many people outside the church are far less racially divided. Consider the military, our places of work, or athletics. Yet there are three places where racial division still persists: bars, prisons, and the American evangelical church.

We need to see the glaring contradiction in saying we believe in hell while making no effort to tear down the walls of racism and ethnic superiority. If we're going to take Jesus' words seriously, we have to make a more concerted effort to forge avenues of racial reconciliation and unity under the banner of the gospel of Christ. One day, Christ will come back and there will be an amazing worship celebration—with African bongos, Indian sitars, and an ensemble of Mariachi trumpets—where every tribe, tongue, nation, and color will bow the knee to their King and *celebrate!* If this sounds irritating, then go back and read Matthew 8. It's written for you.

## Blessed Are the Poor

And what about the poor? While Jesus is ambiguous at times about the nature and duration of hell, He's crystal clear about the necessity of reaching the poor. Yet many hellfire preachers are overfed and overpaid, living in luxury while doing nothing for the majority of Christians who live on less than two dollars a day.[2] Contrast that with Jesus, who in His longest sermon about judgment made helping the poor a vital criterion of who goes where.

Put simply, failing to help the poor could damn you to hell. I know, I know, everyone wants to qualify this. We want to add all sorts of footnotes to fix Jesus' shaky theology in Matthew 25— justification is by faith, not by works; you don't really have to help literal poor people, etc. But it's ironic that some will fight tooth and nail for the literalness of Jesus' words about hell in this passage, yet soften Jesus' very clear words about helping the poor.[3]

On the flip side, some want to keep the stuff about helping the poor but take hell out of the picture. Sometimes people even take Jesus out of the picture—fighting poverty, they believe, is an inherent virtue whether or not it's rooted in the gospel.

Why do we assume that it must be one or the other? Let's keep the teeth of both truths. There's a literal hell, and helping the poor is essential. Not only did Jesus teach both of these truths, He saw them as necessary and interrelated.

## The Tongue of Fire

James doesn't say much about hell in his short epistle. In fact, the word *hell* only occurs once. But this one instance is directed right at me, a teacher of the Bible. In the context of warning teachers that they will incur a stricter judgment (James 3:1), James says that the tongue is capable of burning up an entire forest (v. 5). "The tongue is a fire," James says, and it is ignited by the fire of hell (v. 6). Again, think teachers, those who stand up and communicate God's Word to God's people. It is for this context that James reserves his only warning about hell. He doesn't warn drunks, thieves, or adulterers about going to hell. No doubt James agrees that sinners of all sorts will go to hell, but for some sobering reason he saves his only explicit—and quite scathing—warning about hell for teachers of God's Word.

The same goes for 2 Peter and Jude. As we saw in the last chapter, these short letters are full of hellfire and emphasize that hell is a place for false teachers—those who claim to be speaking for God but are really only speaking for themselves. According to Peter and Jude, these teachers are among us, exploiting us with false words. They indulge the flesh, despise authority, are greedy and hypocritical—and they lead many astray. They speak a lot about God, but the gods they really delight in are their own bellies and wallets. Peter and Jude say they are heading for hell.

## Lukewarm and Loving It

The most terrifying images of hell occur, as we have seen, in the book of Revelation. But let's remember the context in which John writes this book. This isn't an evangelistic tract written for unbelievers— the hell passages here weren't designed to make converts and scare people into the kingdom. They were designed to warn believers to keep the faith in the midst of adversity. In fact, the descriptions of hell in Revelation 14 and 20—21 were first written with the seven churches of Revelation 2—3 in mind. In these churches, there were those who had left their first love (Rev. 2:4), followed the heresy of false teachers (v. 20), and become complacent and "lukewarm" because of the earthly wealth they hoarded (3:15–17). It is to these types of people—people who confess Jesus with their lips but deny Him by their actions—that God reserves the most scathing descriptions of hellfire and brimstone.

I hate to sound as if I'm always singling out the church in America, but it's where I live. And I have seen enough of His church in other countries to know that not everyone lives like us. In fact,

few do. We have become dangerously comfortable—believers ooze
with wealth and let their addictions to comfort and security numb
the radical urgency of the gospel. What's encouraging is that there
seems to be a growing number of American believers who recognize
this and are making changes. Be encouraged by the statement Jesus
made while addressing the church in Sardis. He addresses the "few"
who refused to succumb: "You have still a few names in Sardis,
people who have not soiled their garments, and they will walk with
me in white, *for they are worthy"* (Rev. 3:4).

I would love for Jesus to grace me with those words: *You are
worthy.* Wouldn't you?


## Lord, Save Us


Racism, greed, misplaced assurance, false teaching, misuse of wealth,
and degrading words to a fellow human being—these are the things
that damn people to hell? According to Scripture, the answer is yes.

Let's not miss the very purpose for these lively warnings. God
wants us to do more than intellectually agree with the words of
Scripture: He wants us to live in light of them. Like the ER doctor
who shocks the dead back to life, belief in hell should rescue our
complacent hearts from the suffocating grip of passivity.

*God, help me overcome my selfishness. I want to love the way You
asked me to.*

*I don't want to say another insulting word to or about another
person, not even jokingly.*

*I want to shock my enemies with Christian love.*

*I want to joyfully sacrifice for the poor, and to see You when I see them.*

*I don't want to fit in anymore.*

*Holy Spirit, save me. Set me apart. Make me worthy.*

## Notes

1.  See Rodney Woo, *The Color of Church: Biblical and Practical Paradigm for Multicultural Churches* (Nashville: B & H Publishers, 2009); Michael Emerson and Christian Smith, *Divide by Faith: Evangelical Religion and the Problem of Race in America* (Oxford: Oxford University Press, 2001).

2.  Among the many books about Jesus and poverty, see Ron Sider's *Rich Christians in an Age of Hunger* (Nashville: Thomas Nelson, 1997).

3.  In the context, Jesus is talking about impoverished Christians, not any poor person. This is clear from Jesus' description of the poor as "these brothers of Mine" (25:40 NASB). In the book of Matthew, the term *brother* is used to describe Jesus' literal brothers or his followers (Matt. 12:46–50). It's never a general description of all people. But this doesn't get the church off the hook. Many, if not most, of the two billion people living on less than two dollars a day are confessing Christians.

# Chapter 6

# "What If God …?"

Now I want to approach the passage of Scripture that has caused me more confusion than any other: Romans 9. The text itself is not confusing. Please read it for yourself. It's fairly simple to understand. What makes it confusing is the "newness" of it. That's a strange thing to say about something that was written almost two thousand years ago. But it's a passage that isn't preached often, so when believers come across it, many find themselves confused. We find ourselves asking, "Is this saying what I think it's saying? If this is true about God, why hasn't anyone told me this before?" Is it because we are embarrassed? Maybe we don't want to admit that we believe in a God who is *so* free to do whatever He wants.

In this chapter, Paul asks a necessary question: What if?

> What if God, desiring to show his wrath and to
> make known his power, has endured with much
> patience vessels of wrath prepared for destruction,
> in order to make known the riches of his glory
> for vessels of mercy, which he has prepared
> beforehand for glory? (Rom. 9:22–23)

What if? What if God decided to do this? What if God, as the sovereign Creator of the universe, decided to create "vessels of wrath prepared for destruction"? And what if He did so in order to "show his wrath" and "make known His power"? And what if it's His way of showing those He saves just how great His glory and mercy is? What would you do if He chose to do this? Refuse to believe in Him? Refuse to be a "vessel of mercy"? Does that make any sense? Would you refuse to follow Him? Really? Is that wise?

"What if?" is a probing question that forces us to face our inflated view of our own logic. It's another way of asking: Just how high is my view of God?

## The Potter and the Clay

For much of this book, we've been discussing some unpopular topics: judgment, wrath, and, of course, hell. If you're like me, there's a part of you that doesn't want to believe these things. But as we discussed in chapter one, the more important question is not whether or not you *want* to, but *could* you believe these things, if in fact God says they are true? This seems to be the very thing that Paul is getting at in Romans 9:22–23.

Notice that Paul does not explicitly say that God destroys sinners for the purpose of showing the world just how powerful He is. Rather, Paul simply raises it as a legitimate possibility.[1] In other words, God may want to display His wrath and power by punishing sinners, or He may have some other purpose in mind. Either way, we must come to a place where we can let God be God. We need to surrender our perceived right to determine what is just and humbly recognize that God alone gets to decide how He is going to deal with people.

Because He's the Potter and we're the clay. This, in fact, is the analogy that Paul gives earlier in Romans 9. Paul begins by saying that God will have mercy on whomever He wills and He will harden whomever He chooses (Rom. 9:16–18). These are some very tough statements to swallow, and Paul knows it. That's why he goes on to raise the question that every reader of Romans 9 raises: "Why does he still find fault? For who can resist his will?" (Rom. 9:19). Good question! If God gives mercy to whomever He wants, then why does He still find fault? Or put the question another way: If we all need mercy, and God grants it to some and not others, then who is really responsible—us or God?

But look at Paul's answer to this question:

> But who are you, O man, to answer back to God?
> Will what is molded say to its molder, "Why

have you made me like this?" Has the potter no
right over the clay, to make out of the same lump
one vessel for honorable use and another for
dishonorable use? (Rom. 9:20–21)

Did Paul really just say that?

Does the Potter have the right to do whatever He wants with the
clay? In the midst of the tragedies that life often brings, in the midst
of the mysterious and hidden ways in which God often works, in
the midst of the theological tensions and paradoxes that are woven
throughout Scripture, in the midst of the pain and sorrow and misery and confusion that accompany our existence on earth—we must
come to a place where we can answer yes to this question. *Yes, the
Potter has this right.*

I often hear people say, "I could never love a God who would …"

Who would what? Who would disagree with you? And do
things that you would never do? Who would allow bad things to
happen to people? Who would be more concerned with His own
glory than your feelings? Who would—send people to hell?

But this makes about as much sense as the clay looking up at the
Potter and saying, "I really think you messed up here, let me show
you a better way to mold me." Picture the absurdity! Yet we do it
all the time.

In fact, *I do it all the time.*

It has taken me forty-three years to finally confess that I have
been embarrassed by some of God's actions. In my arrogance, I
believed I could make Him more attractive or palatable if I covered

up some of His actions. So I neglected speaking on certain passages, or I would rush through certain statements God made in order to get to the ones I was comfortable with. The ones I knew others would like.

I am just now seeing the ugliness of my actions. Like the nervous kid who tries to keep his friends from seeing his drunken father, I have tried to *hide* God at times. Who do I think I am? The truth is, God is perfect and right in all that He does. I am a fool for thinking otherwise. He does not need nor want me to "cover" for Him. There's nothing to be covered. Everything about Him and all He does is perfect.

Yet sometimes from our human perspective, it's tough to see exactly how God is perfect and just and good. That's why God says in Isaiah 55:

> My thoughts are not your thoughts, neither are
> your ways my ways, declares the LORD. For as the
> heavens are higher than the earth, so are my ways
> higher than your ways and my thoughts than your
> thoughts. (vv. 8–9)

"My thoughts are not your thoughts." It means we think differently! He hasn't asked us to figure out why He does the things He does. We can't. We are not capable. Our thinking is inferior to His. Let's not think that spending a bit of time meditating on the mysteries of the universe places us on a level that allows us to call God into question. Our God is not a person who is slightly more intelligent: His thoughts are infinitely higher than ours. Knowing that the gap is so large, shouldn't we put our energy toward submitting rather than overanalyzing? It is natural—no, it is *expected*—that there will be times, many times, when you won't figure Him out.


## I Wouldn't Have Done That

And sending people to hell isn't the only thing God does that is impossible to figure out. The Bible is bursting with divine acts that don't make a lot of sense to us.

Think about it.

Early on in the Bible, we read that people have become so evil that God regrets making them. So what does He do? He decides to save some animals and eight of His people—and then He kills the rest. But He doesn't just kill them. He drowns them all with a massive flood (Gen. 6—8).

A flood? He drowns everyone? If I were God, I wouldn't have done that.

Later on, Moses is up on a mountain while the Israelites are down below worshipping a golden calf. When Moses comes down, God commands the Levites to whet their swords and run through the camp and slaughter their brothers and friends and neighbors (Ex. 32:27). Three thousand people died that day, and the Levites were blessed for their obedience! They didn't stop to figure out whether or not the Potter's ways were just.

Years later, God commands the Israelites to slaughter all the inhabitants of Canaan (Deut. 20:16–18). Men, women, and children—*every ... single ... one*. Even though God is merciful, He tells them to take no prisoners. Slaughter them all.

If I were God, I wouldn't have done that.

While the Israelites are conquering the land of Canaan, a man named Achan steals some treasures from the town of Jericho. He lies about it, but when confronted he confesses his sin and returns the items. Nevertheless, Achan and his family—including all of his possessions, tent and all—are all stoned to death as a result (Josh. 7).

If I were God, I wouldn't have allowed that, let alone commanded it.

Many years later, God commands the prophet Ezekiel to do some pretty wild things. Ezekiel is told to lie on his right side for 390 days, to lie on his left side for 40 days, to cook food over human dung, to hold himself back from mourning over his wife's death when God takes her, and to preach sermons laced with sexually explicit rhetoric that would be rated NC-17 were it put to film today.[2]

I definitely wouldn't have done all of that if I were God.

The fact is, Scripture is filled with divine actions that don't fit our human standards of logic or morality. But they don't need to, because we are the clay and He is the Potter. We need to stop trying to domesticate God or confine Him to tidy categories and compartments that reflect our human sentiments rather than His inexplicable ways.

We serve a God whose ways are incomprehensible, whose thoughts are not like our thoughts. Ultimately, thoughts of God should lead to joy, because those same thoughts designed the cross—the place where righteousness and wrath kiss.

Would you have thought to rescue sinful people from their sins by sending your Son to take on human flesh? Would you have thought to enter creation through the womb of a young Jewish woman and be born in a feeding trough? Would you have thought to allow your created beings to torture your Son, lacerate His flesh with whips, and then drive nails through His hands and feet? Parents, imagine it.

I'm almost sure I would not have done that if I were God.

Aren't you glad I'm not God?

It's incredibly arrogant to pick and choose which incomprehensible truths we embrace. No one wants to ditch God's plan of redemption, even though it doesn't make sense to us. Neither should we erase God's revealed plan of punishment because it doesn't sit well with us. As soon as we do this, we are putting God's actions in submission to our own reasoning, which is a ridiculous thing for clay to do.


## Wrestling with God

Yet God doesn't call us to be stoic about our painful experiences. He expects us to wrestle, and He knows that we will experience pain in this life. Life does deal us some heavy blows, and it's natural— *human*—for us to weep, struggle, and cry out in desperation. God calls us to "weep with those who weep" (Rom. 12:15). Even Jesus did this (John 11:35).

Take Job for example. Job was literally the most righteous person in the entire world (the Bible actually says that), and yet he suffered intensely. In a single moment, God took all of his property, his possessions, and even his whole family. And as if this wasn't enough, God allowed Job to suffer from a physical disease—possibly elephantiasis—that produced unbearable pain. His skin became crusty and oozed with puss, his bones burned like fire, and his entire body became deformed.[3] Naturally, Job demanded some answers. He deserved to know what God was doing. He had every cause to sit God down and have Him explain a few things.

Or did he? Again, think Potter and clay.

Job did get his chance to enter the courtroom and plead his case, but when he did, Job quickly discovered that he didn't get to put God on the stand and bombard Him with questions. Instead, Job found himself in the hot seat, and God rebuked him for thinking that he knew better than his Maker: "Where were you when I laid the foundation of the earth?" (Job 38:4); "Have you comprehended the expanse of the earth? Declare, if you know all this" (38:18); "I will question you, and you make it known to me. Will you even put me in the wrong? Will you condemn me that you may be in the right?" (40:7–8); "Shall the faultfinder contend with the Almighty?" (40:2).

In other words, will the clay say to the Potter, "Why did you do this to me?"

What if God, whose wisdom and justice are beyond our understanding, decided to rain down severe suffering upon Job without feeling the need to tell him why? Do you *want* to love a God who would do this? *Could* you love a God like this?

Job did. In fact, after stepping down from the interrogation stand, Job clung to God even more, despite the fact that he never received answers to his questions. Job's response is remarkable: "I have heard of you by the hearing of the ear, but now my eye sees you" (Job 42:5). In other words, Job used to know God from a distance ("by the hearing of the ear"), but now, after having been through the grind and clinging to God when nothing else made sense, Job knew God in a much more intimate way ("now my eye sees you"). And with that, Job arrived at the most important point: It's not about figuring out all of the mysteries of God, but embracing Him and cherishing Him—even when He doesn't make perfect sense to us.

Jeremiah had a similar experience and came to the same conclusion. After the Babylonians ripped through Israel, slaughtering and torturing men, women, and children, Jeremiah threw up his arms and cried out, "You have killed them in the day of your anger, slaughtering without pity" (Lam. 2:21). That's not a typo. You read it correctly. This is exactly what Jeremiah said. *He believed that the actions of the Babylonians were ultimately acts of God.* As Jeremiah looked around and saw a bunch of bodies lying in the street, he said, "God did that."

I almost didn't want to quote that verse. Honestly, as I started quoting Lamentations 2:21, my first thought was, "Don't do it; it's too harsh; it raises too many questions about evil and justice and God's ways; it may turn people off." But then I remembered my confession. God wasn't embarrassed to have Jeremiah write that; it's time I stop being embarrassed by God's actions. His thoughts and ways are infinitely higher than mine. It's time to stop apologizing *for* Him and start apologizing *to* Him.

*Please forgive me, Lord, for wanting to erase all
the things in Scripture that don't sit well with me.
Forgive me for trying to hide some of Your actions to
make You more palatable to the world. Forgive me
for trying to make You fit my standards of justice and
goodness and love. You are God; You are good; I don't
always understand You, but I love You. Thank You
for who You are.*

Jeremiah goes on in his lament to speak of the appalling images of the Babylonian invasion. Starving women eat their own children. Leaders hang by their hands. Children lay dead on the streets because of starvation.[4] There is little in Lamentations that is pleasant. It's a horrifying little book, and aptly titled. If anyone had grounds to "not love a God who would …" it was Jeremiah. He certainly had his doubts and came close to questioning God's justice.[5] But through it all—through tears, pain, confusion, anger, and doubt—Jeremiah clung to the faithfulness and goodness of God, even though he didn't *feel* that God was very good at the moment:

But this I call to mind, and therefore I have
hope: The steadfast love of the LORD never
ceases; his mercies never come to an end; they
are new every morning; great is your faithfulness.
(Lam. 3:21–23)

In the midst of his pain and confusion, Jeremiah clung to the fact that God was God and Jeremiah was not. He let the Potter be the Potter and understood that he was clay.

## His Name Is Tobiah

Throughout Scripture and throughout history, godly women and men have embraced the God of Job and Jeremiah. They held on to a God whom they didn't always understand; a God who is immeasurably good, even though circumstances in life seem to suggest otherwise.

Years ago, I came across an article entitled "Two Minutes to Eternity" by Marshall Shelley, one of the editors of *Christianity Today* at the time.[6] In the article, Marshall tells the story of the miraculous birth of his son. When the child was in the womb, Marshall and his wife, Susan, found out that their child had an abnormal heart and would probably not survive the birth, if he even made it that far. And so the Shelleys wrestled with God. "This was a design flaw," Marshall writes, "and the Designer was responsible." So they prayed. They prayed for a miracle, they prayed for survival, they prayed that the God of all compassion would give the child the breath of life.

Then the day of birth came, and the child was still alive. The child had survived the pregnancy! God is so good! As the child was born, Marshall looked upon his beautiful son: "He was a healthy pink, and we saw his chest rise and fall. The breath of life. Thank you, God."

And then the child died. Two minutes later, their son turned from pink to blue, and he died. The miracle of life was followed by the mystery of death. And as far as the Shelleys were concerned, the Designer was responsible. When the nurse asked the Shelleys if they had a name for the child, Susan responded: "Toby. It's short for a biblical name, Tobiah, which means 'God is good.'"

God is good.

God is good? How could they say that? How could they believe such an unbelievable attribute of God, when everything in that moment seemed to be proving the opposite? Because the Shelleys believed that God is good not only when He makes sense to us, but even when He doesn't. God is good, because God is God. Goodness is inherent in who He is. And the Shelleys believed this. "The name was what we believed, not what we felt," Marshall writes. "It was what we wanted to feel again someday."

And so it is with many things about God that don't seem to add up.

And so it must be with hell.

As I have said all along, I don't *feel like* believing in hell. And yet I do. Maybe someday I will stand in complete agreement with Him, but for now I attribute the discrepancy to an underdeveloped sense of justice on my part. God is perfect. And I joyfully submit to a God whose ways are much, much higher than mine.

## Notes

1.  James Dunn, for instance, says that Paul's statement in Romans 9:22 amounts to the question "Do you think the creature knows better than the Creator?" Dunn goes on to interpret Romans 9:22–23 the same way I do, as suggesting a legitimate possibility yet not offering a dogmatic answer (*Romans* [Word Bible Commentary 38B] [Waco, TX: Word, 1988], 566).

2.  See Ezek. 4, 16, 23, and 24.

3.  See Job 7:5; 13:28; 30:30, 18. The fact that Job's friends could hardly recognize him (2:12) suggests that his body was deformed. The Hebrew word often translated "boils" or "sores" in 2:7 may refer to the disease we now call elephantiasis.

4.  See Lam. 2:11, 20–21; 4:10; 5:11–12.

5.  See for instance 5:21–22, where he seems to question whether or not God will hold true to His promises (cf. Lam. 2:10–21).

6.  Marshall Shelley, "Two Minutes to Eternity," *Christianity Today* 38 (1994): 25–27. I first heard about this story in a sermon by John Piper about ten years ago.

# Chapter 7

# Don't Be Overwhelmed

The thought of hell is paralyzing for most people, which is why we often ignore its existence—at least in practice. After all, how can we possibly carry on with life if we are constantly mindful of a fiery place of torment?

Yet that's the whole point—we shouldn't just go on with life as usual. A sense of urgency over the reality of hell should recharge our passion for the gospel as it did for Paul, who, "knowing the fear of the Lord," persuaded people to believe (2 Cor. 5:11). We should not just try to cope with hell, but be compelled—as with all doctrine—to live differently in light of it.

In fact, Peter makes exactly this point in 2 Peter 3. He describes the Lord's return, the day of judgment, and the destruction of the ungodly. And what does he conclude? That we should throw our hands up in despair because there's nothing we can do about it anyway? No. He asks a pointed question: "Since all these things are thus to be dissolved, what sort of people ought you to be in lives of holiness and godliness?" (2 Peter 3:11).

In light of this truth and for the sake of people's eternal destiny, our lives and our churches should be—no, they must be!—free from the bondage of sin, full of selfless love that overflows for neighbors, the downcast, and the outsiders among us.

In other words, we need to stop explaining away hell and start proclaiming His solution to it.

## A Greater Urgency

Paul's drastic statement in Romans 9 reveals the heart behind his incredible missionary career:

> I have great sorrow and unceasing anguish in
> my heart. For I could wish that I myself were
> accursed and cut off from Christ for the sake of
> my brothers, my kinsmen according to the flesh.
> (vv. 2–3)

Did you catch that? Paul wished he were *accursed*—or sent to hell—so that his fellow Jews could live. That's insane! I don't know what to do with that. I don't want anyone to go to hell, but I would never be willing to go to hell on someone else's behalf! I hate the thought that people around me could end up in hell, but I can't say that I have *great sorrow* and *unceasing anguish* in my heart.

Paul had some frightening things to say about the eternal destiny of those who reject Jesus in this life, but he loved those people like crazy. His life was devoted to seeing them reconciled to God. He even begged people to pursue the healing and salvation that only Jesus offers (see 2 Cor. 5:20).

## More Reason to Rejoice

It's a bit odd that the same Paul who had "great sorrow and unceasing anguish" in his heart commanded us also to "rejoice in the Lord always" (Phil. 4:4). Somehow Paul was able to grieve and rejoice at the same time. This is the tension we live with as followers of Jesus. We are thrilled to know Jesus and be saved from God's wrath, yet we are burdened for our loved ones who don't know Him.

One of the unexpected blessings that came from this study has been a deeper sense of gratitude for the cross. This past Sunday, I attended a worship service at a small church that had no musicians. So we sang some songs with a background track, and others a cappella. In small crowds, I try to sing softly because my voice is not very pleasant. Yet as we sang songs about the cross, I found myself crying out at the top of my lungs.

"TILL ON THAT CROSS AS JESUS DIED, THE WRATH OF GOD WAS SATISFIED!"

I've sung songs like that a thousand times, and I'm sure you have too. But think about that line. Jesus satisfied the wrath of God. This is the same wrath that Jesus, Paul, Jude, Peter, and John spoke and wrote so vividly about. This is the same wrath that is being poured out for your sins. This is the same wrath that ultimately will be satisfied, either in hell or on the cross. We deserve it; Christ endured it. How could I keep from bursting out in joy?

While hell can be a paralyzing doctrine, it can also be an energizing one, for it magnifies the beauty of the cross.

Hell is the backdrop that reveals the profound and unbelievable grace of the cross. It brings to light the enormity of our sin and therefore portrays the undeserved favor of God in full color. Christ freely chose to bear the wrath that I deserve so that I can experience life in the presence of God. How can I keep from singing, crying, and proclaiming His indescribable love?

## Finally ... Are You Sure?

It would make no sense for me to write all I have written without at least asking the question. Are you sure that you have embraced the God who can save you from hell? I don't want to make this all about avoiding hell. As I mentioned earlier, the gospel is far deeper and more wonderful than just that. However, in light of our discussion, it is fitting that I beg you to be absolutely sure that you are not headed there. This is for everyone. Pastors, leaders, seekers, skeptics—no one knows what you are thinking right now. Let down your guard, and take time to deal honestly with the issue.

Do you know Him? Are you secure in Him? In love with Him?

I don't know what your life is like or what hardships you've faced. I don't know what your thoughts on hell are, or whether or not you've been attacked or manipulated with threats of hell in the past. All I know is that from my best understanding of Scripture, hell is a real place for those who choose to reject God. Yet God is not licking His chops looking for any poor soul that He can send to hell. In fact, the opposite is true: "Have I any pleasure in the death of the wicked, declares the Lord GOD, and not rather that he should turn from his way and live?" (Ezek. 18:23; cf. 33:11).

And so we all have a choice before us. Choose life or choose death. God asks you to turn from your ways and live.

Paul addressed a crowd in Lystra with these words:

> "We bring you good news, that you should turn
> from these vain things to a living God, who made
> the heaven and the earth and the sea and all that
> is in them. In past generations he allowed all the
> nations to walk in their own ways. Yet he did not
> leave himself without witness." (Acts 14:15–17)

Again, I don't know who you are or what God has done in your life, but I know He has not "left himself without witness" in your life. Paul says that every single one of us knows the truth about God (see Rom. 1:18–25). In light of this truth, God calls you to respond in love. Turn to God. Embrace Him. Trust Him.

Put your faith in Him. Accept the incredible gift of the cross, where Jesus took upon Himself the punishment we deserve and gives to us the life, healing, and redemption that come only through grace.

I can't think of a better way to end this book than to point you to the words of Paul, who urges us to be reconciled to the God who loves you more than you can possibly imagine:

> We implore you on behalf of Christ, be reconciled
> to God. For our sake he made him to be sin who
> knew no sin, so that in him we might become the
> righteousness of God ... *behold, now is the day of
> salvation.* (2 Cor. 5:20–21; 6:2)

God extends mercy to all *now,* He wants us to know Him *now,* He urges all of us *now* to be reconciled to Him through His Son Jesus Christ. The door is open *now*—but it won't stay open forever.

# Appendix

# Frequently Asked Questions

This book raised many questions about hell; some have been discussed in detail, while others were brushed over to focus on the purposes of this book and in order to keep the book a reasonable length. This appendix is an attempt to answer some of the most frequently asked questions related to the topic of hell.

## Question 1: Are the images of fire, darkness, and worms to be understood literally?

The most well-known imagery used to describe hell is fire. Jesus, for instance, describes hell as the "fiery furnace" (Matt. 13:42), the "eternal fire" (Matt. 18:8–9), and the place where the "fire is not quenched" (Mark 9:48). Likewise, John, in the book of Revelation, depicts hell as a "lake of fire" where the "burning sulfur" torments forever (Rev. 14:10–11; 20:10, 15). Are we to understand these images of fire literally? Will unbelievers literally burn forever, yet never fully be consumed?

Most evangelical Christians who believe that hell is a literal place and that its duration is forever do not interpret the fire imagery literally. Well-known figures such as John Calvin, Martin Luther, C. S. Lewis, Billy Graham, D. A. Carson, J. I. Packer, and Sinclair Ferguson all understand the fire images nonliterally. Other conservative commentators and theologians, such as Charles Hodge, Carl Henry, F. F. Bruce, Roger Nicole, Leon Morris, and Robert Peterson agree. These scholars note that fire imagery is used in many other places in the Bible—not just in passages relating to hell—in obviously nonliteral ways. Jesus says that He "came to cast fire on the earth" (Luke 12:49), which in the context symbolizes judgment. Our Lord didn't literally gather sticks and leaves to set the planet ablaze. John describes Jesus' eyes as like "a flame of fire" (Rev. 1:14); for James, the tongue is a "fire" (James 3:6); and according to Paul, our mundane works will be burned with fire on judgment day (1 Cor. 3:15). Fire is used metaphorically throughout Scripture, and I agree with the host of evangelical scholars above that fire is probably *not to be taken literally when it's used to describe hell.*

This is supported by several passages in which a literal fire would conflict with what the author says elsewhere. Jude, for instance, describes hell as an "eternal fire" (Jude 7), while six verses later he calls hell the "blackest darkness" (Jude 13). Jesus and John the Baptist both describe hell with images of "fire" (Matt. 3:10, 12; 25:41) and "darkness" (Matt. 8:12; 22:13; 25:30). These metaphors of fire and darkness are clearly mixed—where there's fire, there cannot be complete darkness. The mixing of metaphors suggests that these images are just that: *metaphors*. This is further supported by Jesus' statement that hell was created for the Devil and his angels (Matt. 25:41), who are spirit beings. If fire imagery is taken literally, one wonders how fire would work on such non-physical creatures.

Of course God could make all this work. He could prevent fire from penetrating darkness and enable spirits to feel the pain of the flame. But given the widespread use of fire as a metaphor in Scripture, I find it best to take these images nonliterally.

The same probably goes for other images, such as thick darkness (Matt. 8:12; 22:13; 25:30; Luke 13:28), undying worms (Mark 9:43–48), and the gnashing of teeth (Matt. 8:12; 13:42, 50; 22:13; 24:51; 25:30; Luke 13:28). On one occasion, Jesus even says that the unbeliever will be cut into pieces (Matt. 24:51). With such images, I find it best to view them all as powerful ways of conveying the inexplicable notions of punishment that will occur in hell. Fire and the gnashing of teeth depict intense pain and suffering; darkness conveys separation from God; worms that don't die (see Isa. 66:24) probably emphasize the shame of eternal death, if not its never-ending duration.

So while the passages examined in this book are clear about hell as a real place where the wicked will be tormented, the Bible does not seem to tell us exactly what that torment will entail.

## Question 2: Are there degrees of punishment in hell?

Will the Buddhist monk sit next to Hitler in hell? Or will some people suffer a greater degree of punishment than others?

The Bible suggests that there will be degrees of punishment in hell. Jesus said in Matthew 11:24, "It will be more tolerable on the day of judgment for the land of Sodom than for you"—the "you" being those who witnessed the works of Christ. In Luke 12, Jesus tells a parable about some disobedient slaves who receive punishment for their misdeeds. One slave is cut into pieces, another collects many lashes, while the last one gets a "light beating" (vv. 46–48). If this parable applies to punishment in hell, then it affirms that there will be degrees of suffering. Paul also suggests this when he says that unbelievers are "storing up wrath" for themselves on judgment day (Rom. 2:5).

Though Scripture is not crystal clear on the issue, there is support for the view that there will be degrees of punishment in hell.

## Question 3: Is hell at the center of the earth?

Some first-century Jews and many medieval Christians would have said yes. Some books, such as Dante's *Inferno,* suggest this, and such widely read books have a way of creating ideas that seep deep down into the fabric of many cultures. But there is nothing in the Bible that clearly locates hell at the center of the earth.

The Old Testament does say that when people die they go "down to Sheol" (Gen. 37:35). But sheol is not necessarily hell (see question 4), and the reference to "going down" is more of a figure of speech than a geographical designation. Also, as we saw in chapters two and three of this book, "hell" itself is reserved for the wicked *after* judgment day. In other words, no one is in hell right now. They may be in hades (see Luke 16), but hades, like sheol, is where the wicked await their judgment. Hades is not hell.

It's probably best to follow the advice of the early church leader Chrysostom, who said that we shouldn't be concerned about where hell is, only how to escape it. Other than that, we know nothing of its location or geography.

## Question 4: Does the Old Testament word *sheol* refer to hell?

The simple answer is no, sheol isn't hell. The meaning of sheol, often translated as "pit" or "grave," is difficult to translate. The word occurs sixty-five times in the Old Testament, and it describes the place where both the righteous (Gen. 37:35; 42:38; Isa. 38:10, 17–18) and the wicked (Num. 16:30; Isa. 14:19, 11) go after death. Still, this doesn't mean that they go to the same place. It only means that the word *sheol* is flexible and doesn't have to designate the specific destiny of the righteous or wicked. At the very least, sheol is simply a synonym for death; at most, it may refer to some sort of shadowy subhuman existence after death, without specifying the details.

The Old Testament doesn't give us many details about hell. Daniel 12:2 says that the wicked will be resurrected and punished, but no other details are given. Ezekiel 32:17–32 is by far the longest description of the existence of the wicked after they die, but it's a rather ambiguous passage, preventing us from coming to any firm conclusions about the nature of hell. In the passage, Ezekiel seems to make a distinction between sheol (vv. 21, 27) and what he calls "the nether world" (v. 18, cf. v. 24 NASB), where the wicked go when they die. Here, the wicked are arranged according to nationality (vv. 22, 24, 26, 29), where they receive their punishment for what they did while alive. Moreover, it seems that though they are not fully alive, they are fully conscious of what's going on. The wicked receive punishment (v. 27), feel shame (v. 30), and are even "comforted" at the arrival of more inhabitants in this "netherworld" (v. 31). "Misery loves company" seems to be the point here.

Despite what seems to be a detailed description of hell, the genre of the passage prevents us from taking all of these descriptions in a literal manner. At best, we can say that God revealed to Ezekiel that the wicked would receive some sort of punishment after they die. Beyond this, caution must rule our interpretation.

## Question 5: What about the person who has never heard the gospel?

This is a tough one. It comes up in almost every Bible study I've ever taught. What about the man in the jungle who has never heard the gospel and therefore never has the opportunity to accept Jesus? What if he simply responds to the light he's been given? He lived as best he could, and if he had heard the gospel, he probably would have believed it. Will God save such a person?

Everything in me wants to say yes. Because saying yes makes sense. Yes seems fair. But here's the problem: There's nothing in Scripture that says anyone will be saved apart from faith in Jesus.

Scripture also teaches that the so-called "light" we've all been given through creation, what theologians call *general revelation*, is sufficient to condemn but not sufficient to save. In other words, when people look at creation and see that there must be a God, and yet have no way of knowing His name or the plan of salvation, the Bible says that these people do not respond positively to such "light." Paul addresses this directly in Romans 1:

> For the wrath of God is revealed from heaven
> against all ungodliness and unrighteousness of
> men, who by their unrighteousness suppress
> the truth. For what can be known about God
> is plain to them, because God has shown it to
> them. For his invisible attributes, namely, his
> eternal power and divine nature, have been
> clearly perceived, ever since the creation of
> the world, in the things that have been made.
> *So they are without excuse.* For although they
> knew God, they did not honor him as God or
> give thanks to him, but they became futile in

their thinking, and their foolish hearts were
darkened. (Rom. 1:18–22)

    This passage says that all people have been given light—general
knowledge that there is a God—and yet all people reject this knowledge and are therefore without excuse. Even though I have theoretical
stories in my mind of a person living in the jungle who responds
positively to the light he's been given, Paul argues otherwise. This
passage teaches that all people are condemned *not for rejecting the
gospel but for rejecting the "general revelation" that's given to all people.*

    Scripture teaches that a person must come to a saving knowledge
of Jesus Christ to be saved. However, God can reveal knowledge
through many different forms: dreams, visions, or divinely given
thoughts that penetrate the mind of the person living in the jungle,
or whomever. I've heard countless stories, maybe you have too, of
people living in places thick with Islam, or other religions, where
there is little or no exposure to the gospel, and yet people come to
Christ. They have a vision or dream in which Jesus appears to them,
and they respond. God can save whomever He wants, however He
wants, but He always does so through the one avenue He Himself
paved: His Son Jesus Christ.

    I must mention, however, that in Scripture, people are nor-
mally saved through a human messenger. In fact, Romans 10:13–15
indicates that preaching the gospel is the prescribed means through
which God saves people. While God has used dreams and visions
to reach people (cf. Gal 1:12–16), we should not depend on such
means to reach the unreached. There are still 1.5 billion people who

have never heard the gospel. God makes it clear that it is our respon-sibility to go to them.

Everything I've said thus far seems clear to me from Scripture. There are heaps of important follow-up questions that could be asked, but at the end of the day, we have to simply believe what Scripture says and not go beyond it. With all these tough questions, it's best to let God be God and believe that the Judge of all the earth will do right (Gen. 18:25).

## Question 6: Did Jesus preach to people in hell between His death and resurrection?

According to 1 Peter 3, Jesus, "proclaimed to the spirits in prison, because they formerly did not obey, when God's patience waited in the days of Noah, while the ark was being prepared" (vv. 19–20). This is a rather strange passage, but it almost certainly doesn't mean that Jesus was preaching the gospel to unbelievers who had died. The word *spirits,* when used without any qualifications (such as "spirit of man," etc.) refers to supernatural beings, whether good or bad (Matt. 12:45; Luke 10:20; Heb. 1:14). Peter also says that these spirits were disobedient "in the days of Noah." This probably refers to another strange passage in Genesis 6:1–4, where evil angels apparently had sexual relations with women and were "imprisoned" by God for it (see 2 Peter 2:4; Jude 6). This raises many other ques-tions, I'm sure. In any case, it seems that here in 1 Peter 3, Jesus went to that angelic prison and proclaimed victory in light of the cross over these disobedient demons (see Col. 2:15).

So Jesus did not preach the gospel to unbelievers in hell, at least not in an evangelistic sense.

## Question 7: How can God be loving and still send people to hell?

This is a question that many intelligent theologians have wrestled with over the centuries. It was, in fact, this question (among others) that drove the early church leader Origen to believe that all people will end up in heaven. He believed that the love of God demands it.

Can God be loving and still send people to hell? If what I have argued in this book is correct, then we must answer yes. Here are three reasons why:

First, God is love, but He also *defines* what love is. We don't have the license to define love according to our own standards and sensibilities. We often assume that love means achieving the ultimate happiness of everyone you are able to. If this were love, then yes, hell would be incompatible with God's love. But Scripture doesn't define God's love in this way. Love is part of who God is. And God defines what love is. God does not *have* to save everyone for Him to *show love*. Love, in other words, is essentially wrapped up in the character of God. Though God acts in ways that *seem* unloving by our standards, they are not unloving by His standards—and His standards are the ones that matter.

Second, we must understand the love of God in light of His other characteristics. God is love, but He is also holy and just, and He frequently pours out wrath toward sin. In fact, God sometimes withholds certain attributes in order to exercise others. For instance, God withholds His wrath to exercise mercy. God withholds justice to pour out His grace. Of course, God *could* choose to lavish all humanity with His mercy and therefore choose to withhold His wrath toward everyone. But the Bible doesn't support this.

Third, and to my mind most importantly, we must understand God's love in light of God's freedom. As we have seen in this book, God, as the Creator, is free to do whatever He sees best. He is compelled by none other than Himself. And God's freedom means—though it's difficult to swallow—that God *can* withhold love (Rom. 9). It's a logical (and theological) mistake to think that God can't be loving unless He saves everyone. Such an assumption, while seeking to cherish the love of God, violates His freedom and sovereignty.

I'm not at all trying to minimize the pain we feel when we think about the unsaved being tormented in hell, nor am I suggesting that we simply snuff our emotions and move on with our lives: Remember Paul's anguish (Rom. 9:2–3). All I'm suggesting is that as the all-powerful, all-wise Creator of the universe, God does what is just, right, and loving in a much more profound way than we can possibly imagine. We must cling to Abraham's words in Genesis 18:25: "Shall not the Judge of all the earth do what is just?"

# Bibliography

Aune, David. *Revelation 6—16* (Word Bible Commentary 52B). Nashville: Thomas Nelson, 1998.

Bailey, Lloyd R. "Gehenna: The Topography of Hell." *Biblical Archaeologist* 49, no. 3 (1986): 187–91.

Barclay, William. *A Spiritual Autobiography.* Grand Rapids, MI: Eerdmans, 1977.

Bauckham, Richard. *2 Peter and Jude* (Word Bible Commentary 50). Waco, TX: Word, 1983.

————. "Early Jewish Visions of Hell." *Journal of Theological Studies* 41 (1990): 355–85.

————. "Universalism—A Historical Survey." *Themelios* 4, no. 2 (1979): 47–54.

Beale, G. K. *The Book of Revelation: A Commentary on the Greek Text* (New International Greek Testament Commentary). Grand Rapids, MI: Eerdmans, 1998.

Beasley-Murray, G. R. *Jesus and the Kingdom of God.* Grand Rapids, MI: Eerdmans, 1986.

Bell, Rob. *Love Wins.* New York: HarperOne, 2011.

————. *Velvet Elvis: Repainting the Christian Faith.* Grand Rapids, MI: Zondervan, 2005.

Carson, D. A. Matthew (The Expositor's Bible Commentary). Grand Rapids, MI: Zondervan, 2010.

Charlesworth, James H., ed. *The Old Testament Pseudepigrapha.* 2 vols. New York: Doubleday: 1983–1985.

Davies, W. D. and Dale C. Allison Jr. *Matthew* (The International Critical Commentary). Vol. 3. Edinburgh: T & T Clark, 2004.

Dunn, James. *Romans* (Word Bible Commentary 38B). Waco, TX: Word, 1988.

Eller, Vernard. *The Most Revealing Book of the Bible: Making Sense Out of Revelation.* Grand Rapids, MI: Eerdmans, 1974.

Emerson, Michael and Christian Smith. *Divide by Faith: Evangelical Religion and the Problem of Race in America.* Oxford: Oxford University Press, 2001.

Erickson, Millard. *Christian Theology.* 2nd ed. Grand Rapids, MI: Baker, 1998.

France, R. T. *The Gospel of Matthew* (New International Commentary on the New Testament). Grand Rapids, MI: Eerdmans, 2007.

Fudge, Edward. *Fire That Consumes: A Biblical Case for Conditional Immortality.* 2nd ed. Revised by Peter Cousins. Carlisle, UK: Paternoster, 1994.

Garcia-Martinez, Florentino and Eibert Tigchelaar, eds. *The Dead Sea Scrolls Study Edition. 2 vols.* Leiden, The Netherlands: Brill, 1997.

Greggs, Tom. "Exclusivist or Universalist? Origen the 'Wise Steward of the Word' (*CommRom.* V.1.7) and the Issue of Genre." *International Journal of Systematic Theology* 9, no. 3 (2007): 315–27.

Guhrt, Joachim. "Time." In *New International Dictionary of New Testament Theology,* edited by Colin Brown. Vol. 3, 826–33. Grand Rapids, MI: Zondervan, 1986.

Hagner, D. A. *Matthew 14—28* (Word Biblical Commentary 33b). Vol. 2. Nashville: Thomas Nelson, 1995.

Head, Peter. "The Duration of Divine Judgment in the New Testament." In *Eschatology in Bible and Theology,* edited by Kent Brower and Mark Elliott, 221–30. Downers Grove, IL: Inter-Varsity Press, 1997.

Keener, Craig. *A Commentary on the Gospel of Matthew.* Grand Rapids, MI: Eerdmans, 1999.

Lewis, C. S. *The Problem of Pain.* San Francisco: HarperOne, 1940.

Ludlow, Morwenna. "Universalism in the History of Christianity." In *Universal Salvation? The Current Debate,* edited by Robin A. Parry and Christopher H. Partridge, 191–218. Grand Rapids, MI: Eerdmans, 2003.

Luz, Ulrich. *Matthew: A Commentary.* Translated by W. C. Linss. Minneapolis: Augsburg Fortress Press, 2005.

MacDonald, Gregory. *The Evangelical Universalist.* Eugene, OR: Cascade Books, 2006.

Marshall, Howard. "The New Testament Does Not Teach Universal Salvation." In *Universal Salvation? The Current Debate, edited by* Robin A. Parry and Christopher H. Partridge, 55–76. Grand Rapids, MI: Eerdmans, 2003.

Moo, Douglas. "Paul on Hell." In *Hell Under Fire: Modern Scholarship Reinvents Eternal Punishment, edited by* Christopher W. Morgan and Robert A. Peterson, 91–110. Grand Rapids, MI: Zondervan, 2004.

Morris, Leon. *The Gospel According to Matthew* (Piller New Testament Commentary). Grand Rapids, MI: Eerdmans, 1992.

Mounce, Robert. *Matthew* (New International Biblical Commentary). Peabody, MA: Hendrickson, 1991.

Osborne, Grant. *Matthew: Exegetical Commentary on the New Testament.* Grand Rapids, MI: Zondervan, 2010.

Perriman, Andrew. *The Coming of the Son of Man: New Testament Eschatology for an Emerging Church.* Milton Keynes, UK: Paternoster, 2005.

Sasse, Hermann. "*aion, aionios.*" In *Theological Dictionary of the New Testament, edited by* Gerhard Kittel. Vol. 1, 197–209. Grand Rapids, MI: Eerdmans, 1985.

Scott, Mark S. M. "Guarding the Mysteries of Salvation: The Pastoral Pedagogy of Origen's Universalism." *Journal of Early Christian Studies* 18, no. 3 (2010): 347–68.

Sider, Ron. *Rich Christians in an Age of Hunger.* Nashville: Thomas Nelson, 1997.

Talbott, Thomas. "Christ Victorious." In *Universal Salvation? The Current Debate, edited by* Robin A. Parry and Christopher H. Partridge, 15–31. Grand Rapids, MI: Eerdmans, 2003.

———. *The Inescapable Love of God.* Boca Raton, FL: Universal Publishers, 1999.

———. "A Pauline Interpretation of Divine Judgment," In *Universal Salvation? The Current Debate, edited by* Robin A. Parry and Christopher H. Partridge, 32–54. Grand Rapids, MI: Eerdmans, 2003.

Watson, Duane F. "Gehenna." In *The Anchor Bible Dictionary, edited by* David Noel Freedman. Vol. 2. New York: Doubleday, 1992.

Wilkins, Michael. *Matthew* (The NIV Application Commentary). Grand Rapids, MI: Zondervan, 2004.

Woo, Rodney. *The Color of Church: Biblical and Practical Paradigm for Multicultural Churches.* Nashville: B & H Publishers, 2009.

Wright, N. T. "Towards a Biblical View of Universalism." *Themelios*
   4, no. 2 (1979): 54–58.

# About the Author

**Francis Chan** has a BA in youth ministry (The Master's College) and an MDiv (The Master's Seminary). He was in youth ministry for six years and was a senior pastor for sixteen years. In 1994 he started Cornerstone Church, and the church has since established eight additional church plants. He served as senior pastor of Cornerstone Church until 2010. Through Cornerstone, Francis also founded Eternity Bible College in 2004, where he taught and served as chancellor until 2010.

Francis's heart for people is evident through his involvement on the boards of World Impact and Children's Hunger Fund. He travels extensively on mission trips to places like El Salvador, Japan,

Peru, Mexico, and Africa in order to see the needs firsthand and to generate love and support for the people there.

A popular teacher and speaker, Francis addresses tens of thousands of people annually, both in the United States and internationally. His passionate, honest, and unabashed speaking style imprints the truth he shares on his listeners. Typical venues include college chapels, churches, and high school retreats; pastors' conferences such as Catalyst, Orange, and Exponential; and youth conferences such as Passion. *Crazy Love,* a New York Times best seller that has sold over one and a half million copies, was Francis's first book. David C Cook also released the *Crazy Love DVD Study Resource,* based on the book, in January 2009.

His second book, *Forgotten God,* released in 2009 and was followed by the *Forgotten God DVD* and the *Remembering the Forgotten God* workbook. Francis's BASIC. seven-film series, created with Flannel, launched with the first three films *FEAR GOD, FOLLOW JESUS,* and *HOLY SPIRIT.* In addition, he has written three children's books: *The Big Red Tractor and the Little Village, Halfway Herbert,* and *Ronnie Wilson's Gift.*

Francis lives in California with his wife, Lisa, and their five children.

# About the Coauthor

**Preston Sprinkle** has a BA in bible exposition from The Master's College, an MDiv from The Master's Seminary, and a PhD in New Testament from Aberdeen University in Scotland. He has taught biblical studies at Nottingham University in England and at Cedarville University in Ohio, and he currently teaches at Eternity Bible College in Simi Valley, California.

Preston has authored many essays and scholarly articles in publications such as Bible Study Magazine, Journal for the Study of the Old Testament, Journal for the Evangelical Theological Society, Currents in Biblical Research, and many others. He has also worked on three books: *Law and Life*, *The Faith of Jesus Christ* (coedited with

Michael Bird), and the forthcoming *Judaism Revisited*. In addition to teaching and writing, Preston currently serves on the pastoral staff at Cornerstone Community Church in Simi Valley, where he participates in preaching and the global ministry team.

Preston and his wife, Christine, have three daughters and a son. Along with his love for baseball and surfing, Preston enjoys the outdoors—including hiking, camping, and having fun in the sun with his family, as well as hanging out with college students.

*Turn the page to experience …*

**FRANCIS CHAN**

with Danae Yankoski

# CHAPTER 7

# Supernatural Church

*What the soul is in our body, the Holy Spirit is
in the body of Christ, which is the church.*

-Augustine-

I bet you'd agree that a group of talented, charismatic leaders can draw a crowd. Find the right creative team, musicians, and speakers, and you can grow any church. It doesn't even have to be a Christian church. The fact is that without making a conscious choice to depend on the Holy Spirit, we can do a lot. (Although without the Spirit, we wouldn't actually be drawing our next breath—but I am talking about cognizant and intentional dependence on our part.) My point is that a growing and energetic gathering is not necessarily evidence of the Holy Spirit's work.

We all have our natural talents and bents, things that we are "gifted at" (of course, the reality is that those gifts too are ultimately from God). I have friends who are gifted artists, and I love watching them paint and draw. Those of us who are artistically challenged are stunned by the beautiful works of art they create. Others are good with people and can easily work in a variety of jobs that require people skills. Still others know how to sell things, no matter what the product is. And some have the skill set required to pull off a decent church.

A while back I asked my church during a service if they thought I could successfully sell insurance as a career. I did this because I know that some of my natural skills are connected to interacting with people and speaking. The fact is that we all have jobs that come naturally for us. Because of how I was made, I could be an insurance salesman if I had a little bit of training. And I can probably "pull off" a fairly adequate church on my own as well. But who wants or needs that?

I don't want my life to be explainable without the Holy Spirit. I want people to look at my life and know that I couldn't be doing this by my own power. I want to live in such a way that I am desperate for Him to come through. That if He doesn't come through, I am screwed. (I probably shouldn't write that word here, but it's how I truly feel about this.)

There was a time when I got excited over a crowd showing up to hear me preach, but those days are long gone. Now I deeply desire that the Spirit of God would do things that I *know* are not of me and that cannot be faked or accounted for by human reason.

I don't believe God wants me (or any of His children) to live in a way that makes sense from the world's perspective, a way I know I can "manage." I believe He is calling me—and all of us—to depend on Him for living in a way that cannot be mimicked or forged. He wants us to walk in step with His Spirit rather than depend solely on the raw talent and knowledge He's given us.

But instead of living this way, we've created a whole brand of churches that do not depend on the Spirit, a whole culture of Christians who are not disciples, a new group of "followers" who do not follow. If all God asked for were faceless numbers to fill the churches, then we would all be doing all right. Most of us would feel pretty confident. But simply having a good speaker, a service that is short and engaging, a good venue, and whatever else we add to the mix does not make a "good" or "successful" church. God intended for His bride, those who claim His name, to be much more than this.

God is not interested in numbers. He cares most about the faithfulness, not the size, of His bride. He cares about whether people are lovers of Him. And while I might be able to get people in the doors of a church or auditorium if I tell enough jokes or use enough visuals, the fact remains that I cannot convince people to be obsessed with Jesus. Perhaps I can talk people into praying a prayer, but I cannot talk anyone into falling in love with Christ. I cannot make someone understand and accept the gift of grace. Only the Holy Spirit can do that. So by every measure that actually counts, I *need* the Holy Spirit. Desperately.

———————

Sometimes I leave Christian events wondering if we resemble the prophets of Baal in 1 Kings 18 more than Elijah, the prophet of God.

If you've forgotten the story, it may be good to stop here and read that chapter, or else the rest of what I write in this section will make very little sense to you. The prophets of Baal had a loud, passionate worship gathering that lasted from morning till evening. When they were done, they had a great time of fellowship (I think you can call it that). But "no one answered; no one paid attention" (18:29). After all of that, Elijah prayed. God heard his prayer, and fire came down from heaven.

My favorite part of that story comes when it is all over and the prophets of Baal are saying, "The LORD—he is God! The LORD—he is God!" (18:39 NIV). They didn't say, "Elijah is a great speaker" or "Elijah sure knows how to connect with God!" They were stunned by *God*. They were in awe of His power. They knew that what they experienced could not have been manipulated by Elijah. They experienced the power of God.

Is that what happens at the Christian gatherings you attend? Or does it feel more like what the prophets of Baal experienced before Elijah prayed? We can have a great time singing and dancing ourselves into a frenzy. But at the end of it, fire doesn't come down from heaven. People leave talking about the people who led rather than the power of God.

---

This principle carries into the way we live our personal lives as well. People ought to see the transformation in our lives and respond by saying, "The Lord—He is God!"

Has anyone ever been amazed by your peace? Love? Joy? Have they ever envied your self-control? Have you ever prayed that God would so fill you with the Spirit that people would know the change could be empowered only by the Spirit? It is when we are filled with true peace and hope that people notice there is something different about us. The Holy Spirit is the one who gives us both peace (Rom. 14:17) and hope (15:13).

I think we all could agree that living "according to our sinful flesh" is not what is intended for us as children of God. Yet even so, we often choose to face life's issues and circumstances in exactly the same way as someone without the Spirit of God. We worry, strive, and grieve no differently than unbelievers. While it is true that we are humans like everyone else, it is also true that we are humans with the Spirit of God dwelling in us. Yet, whether consciously or not, we essentially say to God, "I know You raised Christ from the dead; but the fact is my problems are just too much for You and I need to deal with them by myself."

Even in our daily living we can look more like the prophets of Baal as we live our lives, running about in a frenzy, trying to fix our problems, not stopping long enough to call on the power of God Almighty. Yet as children of God, we are not called to trust in our idols or ourselves. We are made to be like Elijah, who did not question whether God would show His face that day. He prayed and asked for help, and God sent down fire from heaven in response.

Perhaps you don't need fire from heaven, but peace. Perhaps what you need is wisdom to know which decision to make. Or courage to do the right thing, even though you might lose your job. Or maybe you need love because you feel alone. Or you want people with a similar vision to journey with and support you along the way. Whatever you need, the point is that God is aware of you and your circumstances, and He knows what you really need. He is able to bring these things, people, and circumstances into your life.

But God is not a coercive God. And though He desires for His children to know peace and love and to have wisdom, I have noticed that often He waits for us to ask.

He desires to do more than "help out" a bit. He wants to completely transform us. He wants to take a timid heart and set it ablaze with strength and courage, so much so that people know something supernatural has taken place—life change just as miraculous as fire coming down from heaven. He wants to imbue us with His wisdom because He is the "spirit of wisdom and revelation" (Eph. 1:17; see Isa. 11:2). Even as the Spirit works in us to make us more like Christ, to transform us, He is also patient. This work will not be complete until His kingdom comes in full, though this does not deter Him from working now.

——————

You are most likely familiar with the "fruit passage" in Galatians 5, which says, "But the fruit of the Spirit is love, joy, peace, patience, kindness, goodness, faithfulness, gentleness and self-control. Against such things there is no law" (vv. 22–23 NIV). You may even have the list memorized. But look over those traits right now and ask yourself if you possess each to a supernatural degree. Do you exhibit more kindness and faithfulness than the Mormons you know? Do you have more self-control than your Muslim friends? More peace than Buddhists? More joy than atheists? If GOD truly lives in you, shouldn't you expect to be different from everyone else?

What disturbs me most is when we're not really bothered that God living *in* us has not made much of a noticeable difference. Most churchgoers are content to find a bit of peace rather than a "peace of God, which surpasses all understanding" (Phil. 4:7). We want just enough peace to survive the week (or perhaps even the day).

Certainly there have been times in my life when just getting through the day was possible only with God's supernatural help and presence. You might understand the kind of desperate season I am talking about; most of us have experienced times like this—times when we really do have to ask for peace and sustenance every ten minutes. But what I am talking about is when we live our lives this way, when every day of our lives we are just barely hanging on, looking no different from the rest of the world.

When we exhibit the peace that surpasses the world's under-standing, that's when the world notices. *That's* when people say, "Your Lord—He is God!"

Now, this chapter is not meant to make you feel guilty. But it *is* meant to be a challenge and make a space for you to take an honest look at yourself. Do you know what it's like to be filled with joy? Do you experience genuine peace regardless of your life circumstances? Do you consistently respond with kindness no matter what you receive from others?

Can you imagine what it would be like never to get stressed-out or to worry because you are so filled with the peace and love of God?

Don't you want to be characterized by these attitudes? Don't we all want peace, and self-control, and all the rest?

Notice that the subject ("fruit") in this verse is singular. It does not say that there are many *fruits* of the Spirit, but that one fruit incorporates all the different elements that follow (love, joy, peace, etc.). This certainly doesn't make it any easier.

I don't know about you, but I cannot simply muster up more love. I can't manufacture patience just by gritting my teeth and determining to be more patient. We are not strong or good enough, and it doesn't work that way. None of us can "do goodness" on our own, much less all the other elements that make up the fruit of the Spirit.

But despite our inability to change ourselves in this way, to simply become more peaceful or joyful, we expend a great deal of effort trying. We focus on what God wants us to *do* and forget the kind of people He wants us *to be*.

Instead of mustering up more willpower, let's focus our energies and time on asking for help from the One who has the power to change us. Let's take the time to ask God to put the fruit of His Spirit into our lives. And let's spend time with the One we want to be more like.

I know in my own life I don't just want to do what my mentors do; I also want to spend time with them. I have found that through spending time with those I respect, I become more like them than I would by simply trying to "do what they do." Grunting and saying through clenched teeth, "I *will* be patient!" hasn't worked yet, and that isn't likely to change. But what does effect change is when we begin to ask God to make these fruit manifest in our lives, by the power of His Spirit, and when we spend time in communion with our God.

My favorite verse is quite possibly James 5:17, which reads, "Elijah was a man with a nature like ours, and he prayed fervently." Don't keep yourself from praying desperately and courageously for the Spirit to work in your life simply because you are not the prophet Elijah. As this verse says, Elijah was a human being with a nature like ours. He was just like us. The key thing about him? *He prayed fervently.*

Have you ever thought to yourself, "I'm praying to the exact same God Elijah prayed to"? Do you genuinely believe that Moses, Esther, David, and Daniel had *no* advantage over you spiritually? In fact, some would argue that you have the advantage of both the risen Christ and the indwelling Spirit. Let's stop looking at the godly men and women in Scripture as though their prayer lives are unattainable! Pray fervently, knowing that Peter and Paul and Mary and Ruth were men and women "with a nature like ours" (James 5:17). I know that I tend to run from situations where I *need* God, and I think that is true of almost every one of us. It is safer to avoid situations where we need God to come through than to stake it all on Him and risk God's silence. If Elijah had not had the courage to face down the prophets of Baal that day, if he hadn't prayed fervently and courageously, then he would not have experienced God's power in such a profound way. But in moments of doubt, I can't help but think, *What if God hadn't sent down fire that day and Elijah ended up in the same predicament as the prophets of Baal? What then?*

This is certainly not a call to demand that God prove Himself in each and every circumstance that we manufacture. But it is a profound reminder that God delights in showing up when His people are in desperate need of Him, because that means no one else can steal His glory.

---

Let's delve into the Old Testament once again and look at the story of Gideon in Judges 7. Gideon started with an army thirty-two thousand men strong. In several stages, God purposely dwindled it to three hundred men. I think God did this so that no one could say, "Look what we did!" Instead, everyone knew that it was God's power that defeated the enemy. Only through God could a tiny army of three hundred men rout the much larger Midianite army.

God wants the praise for what we do in our lives. But if we never pray audacious, courageous prayers, how can He answer them? If we never follow Him to positions where we need Him, how can He show up and make His presence known?

Can you, along with Elijah and Gideon, say that when people see your life they respond by praising our Father?

When I live by my own power and strength, relying solely on my natural talents to see me through, then people naturally praise me for how I am living. But when I am living in a way that requires me to depend on the Holy Spirit, people respond by praising my Father in heaven.

---

When was the last time you experienced the hand of God? Ask yourself. Think about the times in your life when you have been touched by God in a way that no one could convince you was a coincidence. These may not be "fire from heaven" or "voice like thunder" kinds of experiences; perhaps it was the wordless whisper of hope when you were overwhelmed by depression. Or perhaps you experienced God through the unconditional acceptance of another human being. Or maybe you glimpsed some of His character through a sunset that just made you stop and worship. We experience God through a variety of means, and God delights to communicate and share Himself with His beloved daughters and sons.

The Holy Spirit is present throughout the New Testament as well as the Old Testament. I believe in Him because I believe the Scriptures. But even if you took away what I "know" about the Holy Spirit from reading the Scriptures, my "right answers" about the Holy Spirit, I would still believe.

I would still believe in the Spirit because I have experienced God the Holy Spirit working in and through and around my life in ways I cannot deny or ignore. I certainly do not advocate ignoring the Scriptures or basing everything on experience, but to completely ignore experience—including your personal experience and the experience of the wider body of Christ, both now and historically—is unbiblical.

If you have not known and experienced God in ways you cannot deny, I would suggest that you are not living in a needy and dependent way. God delights to show up when His children call on His name and when they are trusting fully in Him to come through, whether that is in relationships, in battling sin, in strength to make sacrifices, or in endurance to be faithful in daily life. Are you living this way? Or are you surviving only by your own strength, by your own wits?

## We Were Family

A while back a former gang member came to our church. He was heavily tattooed and rough around the edges, but he was curious to see what church was like. He had a relationship with Jesus and seemed to get fairly involved with the church.

After a few months, I found out the guy was no longer coming to the church. When asked why he didn't come anymore, he gave the following explanation: "I had the wrong idea of what church was going to be like. When I joined the church, I thought it was going to be like joining a gang. You see, in the gangs we weren't just nice to each other once a week—we were family." That killed me because I knew that what he expected is what the church is intended to be. It saddened me to think that a gang could paint a better picture of commitment, loyalty, and family than the local church body.

The church is intended to be a beautiful place of community. A place where wealth is shared and when one suffers, everyone suffers. A place where when one rejoices, everyone rejoices. A place where everyone experiences real love and acceptance in the midst of great honesty about our brokenness. Yet most of the time this is not even close to how we would describe our churches.

Without the Spirit of God in our midst, working in us, guiding us, and living and loving through us, we will never be the kind of people who make up this kind of community. There is no such thing as a real believer who doesn't have the Holy Spirit, or a real church without the Spirit. It's just not possible. But what is possible is that we would individually and corporately quench and hinder the Spirit's activity in and through our lives.

As for me, I am tired of talking about what we are going to do. I am sick of talking about helping people, of brainstorming and conferencing about ways we can be radical and make sacrifices. I don't want to merely talk anymore. Life is too short. I don't want to speak about Jesus; I want to know Jesus. I want to be Jesus to people. I don't want just to write about the Holy Spirit; I want to experience His presence in my life in a profound way.

---

A few months ago, the elders at Cornerstone Church began to ask the question "Why don't we live like the believers who made up the first church?" In Acts 2:42–47 we read the following:

> They devoted themselves to the apostles' teaching and to fellowship, to the breaking of bread and to prayer. Everyone was filled with awe at the many wonders and signs performed by the apostles. All the believers were together and had everything in common. They sold property and possessions to give to anyone who had need. Every day they continued to meet together in the temple courts. They broke bread in their homes and ate together with glad and sincere hearts, praising God and

enjoying the favor of all the people. And the Lord
added to their number daily those who were being
saved. (TNIV)

What followed was a beautiful time of sharing as our elders laid
"everything" at one another's feet. We surrendered the keys to our
cars, homes, and bank accounts. The elders looked me in the eyes
and said, "What's mine is yours. If anything ever happens to you, I
will support and care for your kids *as much as* I would care for my
own. I will be your life insurance." And because they had a history of
genuine sacrifice for the sake of the gospel, I believed what they said.

From there, we began going to some of our friends in the
congregation and expressing our commitment to them. And now
this mentality is spreading. New life is permeating the church as
individuals back up their words with sacrifice. Cars and homes are
being sold or given away. Expensive vacations are joyfully replaced
with caring for others. People are being welcomed into others'
homes—not only for meals, but to live. This is a small example
of the kinds of things that happen when people start to walk with
the Spirit and ask the Holy Spirit to affect every part of their lives.

I just shared about what a few people in one church in one
city in one country are doing. What else might it look like when
people begin to walk with the Spirit, submitting everything to
Him? Dream a little with me. This will look different in various
cultures around the world. The Spirit will lead believers in Beijing
to do different things from believers in the United Kingdom or
Argentina.

This is just a hint of what happens when we begin to actually

SUPERNATURAL CHURCH                                          195

live like we need the Spirit. For us at Cornerstone Church, it is only
the beginning.

## Forceful or Forced?

When I read the book of Acts, I see the church as an unstoppable
force. Nothing could thwart what God was doing, just as Jesus
foretold: "The gates of hell shall not prevail against it" (Matt. 16:18).
The church was powerful and spreading like wildfire, not because
of clever planning, but by a movement of the Spirit. Riots, torture,
poverty, or any other type of persecution couldn't stop it. Isn't that
the type of church movement we all long to be a part of?

So much of what we see today is anything but unstoppable. It
can easily be derailed by the resignation of a pastor or an internal
church disagreement or budget cuts. Churches we build only by our
own efforts and not in the strength of the Spirit will quickly collapse
when we don't push and prod them along. I spent years asking God
to be part of whatever I was doing. When I read the book of Acts, I
see people privileged to play a part in what God was doing.

Recently we held a discussion about how to solve some of the
evident problems in our church. One of our pastors spoke up and
said, "I think we're trying too hard." He went on to share of the
supernatural things that had taken place through his prayer life. At
that point, we decided to stop talking and thinking. The next hour
was spent intensely in prayer. We never got "back to business" that
day. While there is a time to brainstorm and think and act well using
the gifts God has given us, far too often we never get to prayer (much
less start, end, and allow it to permeate all that we do). Let's pray that

God would build His church, an unstoppable force, empowered and sustained by the Holy Spirit.

No matter where you live and what your days look like, you have the choice each day to depend on yourself, to live safely, and to try to control your life. Or you can live as you were created to live—as a temple of the Holy Spirit of God, as a person dependent on Him, desperate for God the Spirit to show up and make a difference. When you begin living a life characterized by walking with the Spirit, that is when people will begin to look not to you but to our Father in heaven and give Him the praise.

My prayer as I've written this book is that it would not merely add to your knowledge. Maybe that sounds strange, but I mean it. Often in Christian circles we talk about truth in lieu of applying it to our lives. We hear an incisive sermon, discuss at lunch afterward how "great" or "powerful" it was, and then never think about it again, much less allow the Spirit to change us through it. The truth is that greater knowledge does not necessarily equal greater spirituality. Knowledge can lead to greater intimacy and a deeper relationship with God, but this is not an automatic effect.

Our Scriptures teach that if you know what you are supposed to do and you don't do it, then you sin (James 4:17). In other words, when we stock up on knowledge without applying it to our lives, we are actually sinning. You would think that learning more *about* God would be a good thing … and it can be. But when we gain knowledge *about* God without responding *to* Him or assimilating

His truth into our lives, then it is not a good thing. According to the Bible, it's sin.

May we not merely gain knowledge. Instead, as we learn, may we grow and confess and change more into the people we've been created to be by the power of the Holy Spirit, who dwells within us. "For the kingdom of God is not a matter of eating and drinking but of righteousness and peace and joy in the Holy Spirit" (Rom. 14:17).

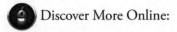 Discover More Online:

www.ErasingHell.com
www.CrazyLoveBook.com
www.ForgottenGod.com
www.BasicSeries.com